Kenneth W. Th_____
been vice presi____
dation, _____
pacities, _____
Sciences, s_____
the politica___
western Uni____
Chicago, from
degree in politic
relations. Dr. The
number of books, 1.
*and the Dilemmas o*___
Political Realism ana
Politics (1960), *Amer__*
Emergent Patterns (1962___
with Hans J. Morgenthau,
*Problems of International I*__
*The Moral Issue in Statecr*__
Dr. Thompson's Rockwell Lectu___
at Rice University.

THE
ROCKWELL LECTURES
1965

Other Published Lectures in This Series

THE MORAL ISSUE
IN STATECRAFT

THE MORAL ISSUE
IN STATECRAFT

———

*Twentieth-Century
Approaches & Problems*

KENNETH W. THOMPSON

LOUISIANA STATE UNIVERSITY PRESS

CONTENTS

INTRODUCTION

PUBLIC discussion in the 1960's of America's responsibilities in the world concentrates heavily either on events of the immediate past and present or, less frequently, on the shape of the distant future. Leaders and citizens repeatedly call upon one another to account for current policies or past failures or to map out long-term national goals and programs. By contrast, scholars and interpreters pay little attention to the immediate future or to that broad intermediate range which makes up the stream of history over the years that lie just ahead. All too little is being written about the problems that have not yet found their way to the desks of the secretary of state or other responsible officials, nor is enough being said about the mood and spirit in which leaders must grapple with such issues. If a hard pressed official turns to the sources of the country's political and intellectual leadership, he is engulfed by a flood of specific proposals for solving the problems of Vietnam, Berlin, or the Congo. But if he seeks advice and counsel about future Vietnams or the framework within which they should be considered, he can expect a much smaller response.

This study is partly addressed to such a need. The goal is not to advance a body of dogmas. It is possible, of course, to argue that what we lack is a doctrine of foreign policy to inform and guide decision-makers. How often are we not told that our policies are bereft of principle, that we have little sense of national purpose, and that as the comparatively recent inheritor of world leadership we flounder for want of a national tradition. If signposts are missing along the way, the cause is the lack of a sense of direction. There are those who would fill the void with a design for victory, or new strategic doctrines, or a new creed of freedom.

A more modest view might be to suggest that the American republic is more richly endowed than its critics imagine. At the core of its founding and history is a moral and political tradition representing what Walter Lippmann has called "the forgotten foundations of democracy." But if the foundations have been forgotten, they have never been lost. Moreover, they affect foreign policy, for as the brilliant diplomatic columnist James Reston has pointed out, "The liberties which all the spokesmen at the White House, the State Department and the Pentagon talk about defending today, after all, were established by that remarkable group of [eighteenth] century American political leaders who took their conception of man from the central religious tradition of Western civilization." At a time when most of the discussion of statecraft centers around nuclear strategy or hard bargaining, this historic fact justifies a review and analysis of the moral issue. The persisting lesson of the eighteenth- and early nineteenth-century chapter in the unfolding of this tradition was the willingness of "that remarkable group" of leaders to apply moral principles to the emerging issues of government. Thus, new political institutions, laws for safeguarding inalienable individual rights, and external policies reflected moral principles of that day. In the same way, the countless issues and problems that face Americans abroad may be illuminated by what I have called the Anglo-American approach. This approach is an essential resource for those who view problems of the present, the intermediate future, and the more distant future.

Chapters I and II are devoted to a survey of the Anglo-American approach viewed from the standpoint of certain underlying issues and then as expressed by intellectual and political leaders. Among them, some undertake to read the future; I have called them the prophets of this approach. Others—responsible political leaders—exemplify the tradition in what they have said and done as practitioners of statecraft. Part I also includes an examination of selected unsolved problems in which the moral issue may be seen in particularly vivid and acute terms.

Chapter III views the moral issue in the context of change. In it I consider, first, the changing dimensions of politics and morality, keeping in mind what is enduring and permanent and what may be subject to adaptation, further elaboration, and change. In this section I have placed the emphasis primarily on the present and the relatively near future. In "A View from the Twenty-first Century," I venture still further onto uncertain ground in seeking to anticipate some of the issues and situations that lie ahead.

Throughout the book I have tried to keep my eye on the target of identifying and assessing the changing future from the standpoint of moral problems and issues. This is not the only possible perspective for viewing present and future problems. However, it is one of sufficient moment to warrant one further contribution to a long and respected—if sometimes interrupted—stream of thought.

Chapter V attempts to assess and evaluate the moral and religious resources which affect the pursuit of the moral issue in statecraft. It reviews the inevitable and inescapable tension existing in the relationship between morality or religion and politics. It examines the comparable relationship between science and morality and points up the painful, complicated areas of moral choice that were ushered in by modern science. Finally, it summarizes the basic issues which confront mankind in relating Christianity and religion to social problems. This section is intended to provide some tentative conclusions about the moral issue in statecraft.

THE MORAL ISSUE
IN STATECRAFT

I

THE ANGLO-AMERICAN APPROACH

Essential Precepts
and Problems

They were the pillars of the temple of liberty; and now that
they have crumbled away that temple must fall unless we,
their descendants, supply their places with other pillars, hewn
from the solid quarry of sober reason.
LINCOLN ON THE "FOUNDING FATHERS"

We should take from the past its fire and not its ashes.
JEAN JAURES

THIS is a book about the moral issue in politics and foreign policy. The nature of international society provides assurance that there must be a moral issue. For in contrast to organized local and national communities which have achieved some degree of consensus on law or morality, the worldwide community is divided by political ideologies, contending nationalism, differing religion, and race. The context of a barely emergent world community sets limits to the application of common moral principles. Ideals and principles mean different things for Communists and democrats. Goals such as peace and justice are measured by aims and national interests that are not the same.

Each side in the present struggle between communism and democracy is prone to interpret the other's conduct as a cynical abandonment of principle. Yet, the principle by which the adversary is judged is usually the critic's, not the practitioner's.

Nevertheless, we know that nations, like individuals, are seldom immune from ethical considerations. Because they are human and participate in mankind, they ask themselves what is right and wrong. Communists justify their policies not by outright condemnation of the ends of democracies, but by claims that they represent a higher form of democracy. They call themselves "people's democracies." Democracies in turn deny that they neglect equality and social justice—the highest goals in the Communists' scale of values. Indeed, it is possible to argue that the Western democracies have overturned the Communist prediction of a worldwide social revolution by achieving social reforms that extend the benefits of developed economies to all their people.

In foreign policy, moral principles are generally applied within a restrictive context. Nations affirm loyalty to treaty commitments and the rules of international law but in practice apply them in accordance with national interests. The rules of international law are binding within the limits of each country's pursuit of its national security. The responsibility of statesmen to speak the truth is practiced up to the limits of disclosing information that may damage programs of national defense.

The moral issue results from the context in which international morality is practiced. Statesmen can afford neither to disregard the context nor to be scornful of objective standards of right and wrong. The most towering idealists must understand the context and setting of international problems. The most cynical realist cannot afford even in the interest of realism to ignore political ideals. Even those statesmen who have scoffed at the higher principles undergirding the United Nations have been obliged to amend their harsh criticisms. For man is at heart a moral being.

The moral problem arises from the fact that statesmen deal not with one moral principle but many. Western leaders stand for peace but also for self-determination and freedom. They espouse the goals of Western civilization while sharing the aspirations of the new nations. Morality is more complex in international politics because of the great variety of aspirations and purposes among states. The moral problem is further intensified by the uncertainties of applying different values in situations that are commonly in flux and the unpredictability of the consequences that will flow from political actions.

These factors have prompted me to explore a broad range of situations and problems in search of relevant moral principles. The test of this approach will be whether it illuminates the international situation, and more particularly international morality.

Historians looking back on nearly two centuries of American foreign policy in search of the moral issue note two divergent trends of thought. One puts stress on understanding the world as it is without speculating about what it ought to be. The other places its emphasis on conceiving and bringing into being a new and better world. Both strains persist throughout our history. Each helps us to think about moral problems. For try as we will to be utterly realistic or wholly idealistic, few among us can escape the pulls and constraints of these countervailing forces. We must live in the world while dreaming dreams about the future. The test is whether we see reality clearly and see it whole without losing sanity and hope.

Everyone must accept himself as a person fashioned through and through by ambitions, drives, vitalities, and limitations. My neighbor shares with me the burdens and opportunities of being human, but my neighbor and I are not the same. He may be strong where I am weak. His prospects of success may match mine of failure. Yet, if my strengths and weaknesses are laid alongside his, I too have a niche I can fill. "Know thyself" is still the best guide to human adjustment; but this requires clarity, courage, and a sense of humor. Man is endlessly tempted to imagine that he is more than man, or at least more than himself; and this is the source of his glory and despair. Most of us live out our years testing whether we stand at the point of abject hopelessness or supreme grandeur; somewhere between them we find a piece of ground that is our own whatever the future may bring. Each of us has a destiny, but each must learn that he is not God. At the center of life is a running contradiction: man is both greater and less than he imagines himself to be.

The same is true of the larger communities in which men live. Nations are abstractions with a life of their own made up of the lives of past, present, and future generations. It is futile to argue about their reality apart from that of individuals. From birth to death, men are profoundly affected by whether they are Americans, Englishmen, Russians, or Chinese. Nationalism in the broadest historical sense provides the context of existence. It may be a passing phase in the organization of mankind, but for the present it remains powerful and pervasive in the order of things. It shapes educational systems, sets the framework of values and goals, and determines political, social, and economic arrangements. Nationalism is unquestionably a myth, but a myth which dominates existence.

American nationalism is illustrative, not contradictory, of this truth. It provides the context within which an American can talk about the moral issue. From the beginning of the American republic, dream and reality cohered in the national experience. The first chapter in American history is particularly rich because the founding fathers were acutely sensitive to the relationship between purpose and politics. On one side, they had a pervasive sense of national destiny—a sense carved out of the traditions of Western civilization and thought. "Providence," according to Jonathan Edwards, "intended America to be the glorious rennovator of the world." The new nation was the home of God's "chosen people," who had thrown off the miseries and travail of Europe. They were done with petty quarrels and ancient rivalries. They had shaken the dust of the Old World from their feet and by force of arms and national resolve had freed themselves from colonial tyranny. Here there was a chance to test and realize the noble purposes of liberty and equality professed abroad but denied in practice. In Ralph Barton Perry's words, "It would be American to improve and modernize Heaven rather than to enjoy it for a static eternity." Alongside the stirring beliefs of freedom and justice, however, our early leaders grasped the unavoidable connection between American policies and European events. Even the most towering of earlier, classical, utopian writings had recognized the dependence of national security on prudent policies and geographical advantage. For utopians such as More, Tommaso Campanella, and Johann Valentin Andreae, the ideal state was the island state. And the latter, writing in *Christianopolis* at the beginning of the Thirty Years' War (1618–48), could declare, "Not even the most pious can live in peace, when it does not please the wicked neighbor." In this awareness, utopians and realists join hands, for Andreae's terse phrase is reflected in Winston S. Churchill's tart warning: "When wolves are about the shepherd must guard his flock even if he does not himself care for mutton."

NORMS AND REALITIES

In their quest for security, American colonists were not unmindful of the need to placate or resist friend and foe on American soil. As late as 1775, they saw their destiny linked with the success of Britain's policies. In the address of the First Continental Congress to the people of Great Britain on October 21, 1774, they acknowledged the protection they had received from the motherland: "Did we not, in the last war, add all the strength of this vast continent to the force which repelled our common enemy? Did we not leave our native shores, and meet disease and death, to promote the success of British arms in foreign climates? . . . We shall consider your enemies as our enemies, and your interest as our own. . . ." Only when the appeal to common liberties and common interests failed did Benjamin Franklin, Thomas Paine, and John Adams turn from Britain to France. In calling for France's assistance, the colonists appealed less to common liberties than to common interests. In March of 1776, John Adams asked: "Is it the interest of France to stand neuter, to join with Britain, or to join with the Colonies? Is it not her interest to dismember the British Empire? Will her dominions be safe, if Britain and America remain connected?" When independence came, it was France and Spain who aided the American colonials, less from common ideology than common political cause.

With independence, there were forces that drew America apart from Europe. Geographically, it most nearly approximated the utopians' vision of an island state. The goal of a new society uncorrupted by ancient practices like the European balance of power coincided with hardheaded national interest. Isolation was both morally and politically superior to any other course. The practical basis for isolation has seldom been more cogently stated than in John Adams' observation to the British plenipotentiary Oswald during the peace negotiations in November, 1782: "It is obvious that all the powers of Europe will be continually maneuvering with us, to work us into their real or imaginary balances of power. . . . They will all wish to make us a makeweight candle, when they are making out their pounds. . . ." The policy of no entangling alliances evolved to meet circumstances. A newly independent state needed time and freedom from outside interference to organize a government and carry forward national development. With the British threat to Louisiana and the Floridas in 1790, Thomas Jefferson warned, "The later we interfere, the better shall we be prepared."

Soon he saw that freedom from the struggle was impossible. At first, he seemed convinced that "an English ascendancy on the ocean" was desirable. Later, he found himself "under the necessity of wishing success to Bonaparte" and declaring "Down with England." But with the march of Napoleon across Europe, he feared the conquest of Russia and the domination of Europe, including England, by France. "Put all Europe into his [Napoleon's] hands, and he might spare such a force . . . as I would leave not have to encounter. It cannot be to our interest that all Europe should be reduced to a single monarchy." Thus, it was not the doctrine of isolation that Jefferson invoked but the assurance "that a salutary balance may ever be maintained among nations and that our peace, commerce, and friendship, may be sought and cultivated by all." A balance of power and the participation of the United States in the politics among nation-states had become at that time the precondition of American national security. But Jefferson's emphasis was to shift again at the time of the Monroe Doctrine when he found European interests "entirely distinct from ours. Their mutual jealousies, their balance of power, their complicated alliances, their forms and principles of government, all are foreign to us."

Jefferson and a long procession of statesmen who followed him were ambivalent about the connections between norms and realities. They saw the laws of nature and nature's God mirrored in their experiment of freedom. Is it surprising that this required, as they saw it, as much independence as possible from Europe's wars and rivalries? In international politics, however, it is always easier to discover and proclaim general principles than to apply them. The demands of national security competed from the beginning with the general principle of isolation from Europe. Our early leaders were forced, despite bold words to the contrary, to call on successive European powers to help them preserve territorial integrity and national independence. In these instances, nations of the Old World were called on to redress and maintain an equilibrium of forces in the New World even as the New World was later to redress the balance of power in the Old World.

The same conflict between courses of action later nearly destroyed another general principle deeply cherished in the New World. For spokesmen of the Enlightenment such as Jefferson, the French Revolution heralded the dawn of a new era, the final downfall of an ancient evil. Jefferson deplored the shedding of innocent blood by the guillotine; but rather than have the cause of liberty fail, he "would have seen half the earth desolated." A revolutionary fervor swept the United States; the title "citizen" took the place of "mister." In Philadelphia, Louis XVI was hung in effigy twenty or thirty times a day. Passions for France ran high, and the cry for intervention on the side of the French against England sounded through the streets. The Jacobin followers of Citizen Genêt embarked on a twenty-eight-day-long triumphal procession through the back country to Philadelphia. The authority of the government of President Washington was thrown into question. According to John Adams, ten thousand people in the streets of the capital threatened to drag Washington from his house and compel the government to declare war against England in favor of the French Revolution. Judged by the majority view of vocal public opinion, the government pursued a policy that lacked popular support. However, Washington stood firm in his announced neutrality between France and Britain, Genêt went too far, and the tide of history swept on. While in 1793 many Americans had seen absolute right embodied in the French, by the early nineteenth century the United States, with a sweeping revulsion of popular feeling, had instituted the Alien and Sedition Acts. With the publication of the X.Y.Z. dispatches in 1798, anti-French feeling rose to a fever pitch. The treaty of 1778 with France was formally abrogated, and a period of undeclared war against the French Republic followed. A few years later, the pendulum swung back, the anti-French Federalists were voted out of office, and Jefferson became the third President of the United States.

What are the lessons of these turbulent changes? How is it possible to account for the sweeping surges of popular emotion and strong pressures on government? First, these events suggest the great hazards of thinking in terms of absolute right and wrong. It was not that the noble principles of "liberty, equality, and fraternity" were at fault. It was, rather, that nations are obliged to assess complex social and political movements less according to the truths they proclaim and more from the stand-point of changing directions and evolving patterns and ambi-tions of the movements as well as their effects on the national interests of others and on international order. Second, diplomats may not indulge themselves the passions of an aroused public. General George C. Marshall was to observe more than a century later that the first rule for a public servant is to keep down his emotions. In Talleyrand's classic phrase: "Surtout, pas trop de zèle." A contemporary wrote of Cromwell: "You shall scarce speak to . . . [him] about anything but he will lay his hand on his breast, elevate his eyes and call God to record. He will weep, howl and repent, even while he doth smite you under the fifth rib." Third, circumstances and combinations change, new group-ings arise, old interests are replaced by new. Nicholas J. Spyk-man once remarked that the charming thing about international politics was that no one need grow weary of his friends. For is is not self-evident that yesterday's friends have become today's rivals—as with China and Soviet Russia? And that enemies of the past have become allies of today—as with Germany and Ja-pan following World War II? Between the poles of strong rivalry and warm friendship, relations with other states move along a changing front—as our postwar connections with France and India, Pakistan and Tanzania, Indonesia and Ghana, Egypt and Uganda make abundantly clear. Americans must learn to expect these variations in the same way ebb and flows in personal friend-ships are taken in stride.

The analogy between military and political decisions is often questionable. In one respect, at least, the two realms are similar. They both place a high premium on the evaluation of circum-stances, and no handbook provides answers in advance. The test of the military and political leader occurs in his capacity to measure and assess all the factors. While Churchill was speaking of military judgment, it may not be farfetched to apply his principle to political and moral judgments. He wrote:

> Circumstances alone decide whether a correct conventional manoeuvre is right or wrong. The circumstances include all the factors which are at work at the time: the numbers and quality of the troops and their morale, . . . their confidence in their leaders, the character of the country, the conditions of the roads, time and the weather; and behind these the politics of their states. . . . And it is the true comprehension at any given moment of the dynamic sum of all these constantly shifting forces that constitutes . . . genius.
>
> The problem can seldom be calculated on paper alone, and never copied from examples of the past. Its highest solution must be evolved from the eye and brain and soul of a single man, which from hour to hour are making subconsciously all the unweightable adjustments, no doubt with many errors, but with an ultimate practical accuracy.

This requirement sets limits to the great and the near great in statecraft and shows why military, political, and moral judgments are so painfully difficult. It also provides a firm starting point in studying the moral issue.

THE ANGLO-AMERICAN APPROACH

If the context of foreign policy bears some resemblance to the structure of action described above, the question that follows is how will responsible leaders choose to cope with reality? As history makes plain, the options are numerous if not unlimited. Nations confronted with the need to balance moral and strategic imperatives may choose to stand aside from the harsh requirements of international politics. Moral principles, whether of individuals, church, or state, are always more pure and unsullied in declarations than in application. In an age of American innocence when the commitments and responsibilities of international relations were carried largely by others, the voice of America rang clear and true in the halls of world politics. We were against armies, alliances, the balance of power, European imperialism, and war. We stood for peace, freedom, and justice.

We sought to isolate America from the world of struggles and to preserve national virtue. The so-called neutrals assumed a similar mantle of self-righteousness following World War II. They were as pure in the mid-twentieth century as we had been in the late eighteenth and nineteenth centuries—up to the point where they were threatened by Chinese imperialism or confronted by the needs of balancing policies of disarmament and national security. Even then they fell back on moral pronouncements.

If one way of dealing with the real world involves withdrawal and moralism, another is based on cynicism and hard utopianism. The American people have never been at ease with the latter approach. Its harsh and strident tones have created a profound sense of guilt and national embarrassment. Moreover, the American constitutional system was designed to make certain that those persons who gain political power occupy positions as the nation's servants and not as its rulers. They have, to use a contemporary expression, been on tap, not on top. Not so in societies where military regimes have prevailed or where a general or admiral has won control of a civil regime. There are examples in German history of admirals and generals coming to dominate the thinking of, say, the Kaiser and other instances of kings and potentates who yielded to the military viewpoint. Only in recent times has a retiring American President, Dwight D. Eisenhower, had occasion to warn that the combination of a permanent armaments industry and an immense military establishment constitutes a threat to the "very structure of our society" and that "the potential for the disastrous rise of misplaced power exists and will persist." Not until the post–World War II era have military personnel numbered 3,500,000 of a total of 5,000,000 public servants. The crisis in Vietnam has provoked more uneasiness than any other conflict in modern times that American policy is being determined by a military rather than a political point of view. Yet the American outlook, in contrast to the historic German view, has kept militarism in check. Americans have found bald and unguarded statements about going to the brink of war repugnant and have more recently chosen a President because his rival was said to be trigger-happy. Appeals for preventive wars have not attracted significant followings, and support for the doctrine of the first preemptive strike in a thermonuclear war has generally been confined to a handful of military strategists. American political philosophy has had no major thinker consistently attuned to the harsh philosophy of Nietzsche. The demands for total victory or unconditional surrender have found but limited acceptance and that only in a time of all-out war.

This leaves a third possible approach, one associated most frequently with French rationalism. From Bonaparte to De Gaulle, the quality of unyielding and unequivocal logic has characterized the French world view. Sir Harold Nicolson maintains that this accounts for the relatively modest success of recent French diplomacy. Leaving aside North Africa, French diplomatists have tended to pursue a single logical principle, often beyond the point of no return. The single goal of French grandeur or of a cultural mission in the world has made those Frenchmen who practice diplomacy rigid, inflexible, and poorly equipped for compromise and give and take.

What remains is the traditional outlook of the English-speaking world clinging to goals and purposes but preserving a spirit of patience and restraint in the conduct of policies. Lacking as harsh a view of the world as that espoused by the Germans and holding to a more tentative and pragmatic concept of the future than the French, the British have shared with the Americans a singular approach to reality. Call it idealism tempered with realism or democracy enriched by pragmatism; in either case, its outlines are deeply embedded in British and American culture. If there is an Anglo-American approach, its practice involves variations on a common theme. Implementing it has caused differences that are often greater than similarities and that reflect geographical, economic, and political forces. One partner frequently surpasses the other in sensing the appropriate method of dealing with an issue. The British, for example, have had a surer sense for the uses of power in diplomacy. The Americans have taught their ally that an imperial order, however just, is not just enough to hold back the rise of nationalist aspirations. The conservative tradition in Britain, with its roots in a medieval and aristocratic past, has been a marvelously flexible instrument. But American conservatism all too often overlaps into reaction. In the midst of differences of degree, however, a common core of principles and procedures has evolved; and each member has profited from the experience of the other. This assertion can be tested in the chronology of their relations, in the common moral and intellectual interests of the partners, and in their mutual dependence.

A brief review of postwar American foreign policy may help to measure this relationship. Between the two world wars Americans often exhorted one another to seek peace through international law and novel world institutions. But in the aftermath of World War I many loyal and responsible persons came to feel a deep sense of shame and guilt. While Woodrow Wilson had been the prophet of world law and order, the United States Senate, after his return from the Paris Peace Conference, repudiated the League of Nations. The nation's succeeding generation of intellectual leaders, among them such men as Nicholas Murray Butler and James Shotwell, called for a rededication to world organization and effective world law. Their resolve and conviction, and that of many others, paved the way for American sponsorship of the United Nations and a new International Court.

Perhaps because these international goals were so largely realized in the founding of new international institutions, postwar leaders have concentrated increasingly on another aspect of the United States' responsibility in the world. Recent history makes it clear that new and more orderly forms of international relationships have not altered a basic requirement in world politics. A nation which aspires to world leadership must develop a clear image of its role in the world, of the purposes for which it stands, and of the policies its security and traditions require. It must also obtain the means and power to accomplish its goals. A great power that calls on the world to embrace international values must first enunciate its own national values and then clearly relate those values to worldwide and universal ones. In the eyes of the world, the United States is frequently less successful in articulating working national purposes than in formulating broad international goals. Even friendly critics abroad point to the gap between what we say and what we do. The annals of inter-state relations clearly attest that other world leaders, from the time of the Roman Empire to the British Commonwealth, share with us the dubious privilege of being objects of continuing widespread criticism. However, shortcomings and the apparent inevitability of attacks will not excuse us from making guidelines for United States' conduct in the world.

Stated another way, goals and policies must be related to the facts of the international situation. The facts which dominated the immediate postwar scene were the devastation of Europe and Japan, the decline of ancient empires, and the rise of two great new centers of power—one in the east and the other in the west. As one emerging center of worldwide power, the United States found itself catapulted into a responsibility it neither sought nor was prepared to fulfill. It was called upon to exercise global in-fluence in the interests of restoring international order and pro-viding for the maintenance of peace. Britain had the benefit of four centuries of experience and more than a century of national supremacy in the evolving of Pax Britannica. A similar period of testing was denied the new leader of the West.

Indeed, for more than a century America had proved itself singularly inept in coming to terms with the harsh problem of responsibility and power. This was not for want of good inten-tions or lofty and worthy purposes. Instead, there was a lack of clarity in the functions of morality in world politics and the costs of responsibility. Beginning as early as 1840, there were organized expressions of public feeling proclaiming deep-seated suspicion of both diplomacy and force. The peace movement which developed in the late nineteenth century as a public reaction to war had as its goal the substitution for power of legal procedures like arbitration—which was the first expression of the peace movement to receive governmental sanction—and other forms of moral suasion.

Arbitration had served nations well at the turn of the century on issues which had not proved amenable to diplomacy. Settlements such as those reached in the *Alabama* claims case and the Bering Sea fisheries dispute were fresh in the public mind; and it was not surprising that the question should be asked, why, if settlements like these had been possible, could not the same principles be applied to resolve all differences? Those who asked the question forgot that states reserve to themselves decisions on matters where vital interests are at stake. The United States itself had refused arbitration on the issue of the sinking of the *Maine*, which touched off the Spanish–American War; and no thoughtful person could have imagined the United States agreeing in advance to bind itself to arbitrate problems involving the Monroe Doctrine or strategic interests in Panama or the Caribbean.

The problems of power have obviously been magnified by the sharp rise in the magnitude of force. Nearly four decades ago British Prime Minister Herbert Asquith observed that science was beginning to "lisp the alphabet of annihilation." The dangers are daily borne in upon us not only of mutual devastation in war but also of radioactive poison in peace. Yet in the hydrogen era our approach to the problem of force has been curiously reminiscent of earlier days. The number of words and proposals devoted to a generalized attack on the disarmament problem exceeds attention given to any other problem. Whereas before World War II the approach was one of erecting a system of fixed legal and arbitral procedures culminating in broad, overall, international legislation outlawing war—the Kellogg–Briand Pact

—the postwar design has called for almost endless exchanges of talk with Soviet delegates within the United Nations and outside, all looking toward the banning of the use of force, at least in certain of its forms, or to its control and regulation. It may be significant that the only measurable progress in arms control has come through bilateral negotiations between the United States and Russia.

If the present crisis between East and West were a simple clash either of military systems or political ideologies, we could doubtless speak with greater assurance about the future. However, because of the dual nature of the Soviet threat, we tend to vacillate between a military and an ideological view of the struggle. The problem of arriving at valid and acceptable policies is basically the problem of defining the nature of the crisis. The uncertainty we feel about policies is really an uncertainty over the crisis. There is irony in this perplexity because many informed observers in the early days of the cold war were convinced that the Russian threat to western civilization was identical with the Nazi menace. Thus, men assumed the recipe for dealing with it was the same. It was said that if our leaders had learned anything from more than two centuries of national experience, it was that foreign policy divorced from strength is impotent—a lesson not shared by all the people.

Seen from this approach, the immediate military threat can be interpreted as unquestionably the gravest danger. Those who hold this view call for ever greater urgency in the multiplication of more powerful weapons of destruction, for new strategic doctrines, for hardened missile bases, and for a growing nuclear weapons pool. The irreconcilable conflicts and tensions of the cold war will come to an end only when one side or the other forges decisively ahead. This trend of thought prompts a state to bestow the most lethal weapons on its allies and to continue to produce larger and larger numbers of such weapons.

Some of our friends abroad have warned against too much preoccupation with armaments, especially in light of their suicidal nature. However, the contradictory reactions in the new states to thermonuclear devices are best seen in the effects of the sputniks. In the same countries that repeatedly urge disarmament, American prestige and virtue suffered a grievous blow when the Soviet Union launched the first satellite. Despite continuous criticism of America throughout Asia and Africa for its bland materialism and its preoccupation with purely technological and military advance, confidence in American policy is gauged by the standards by which, in another context, our conduct has been deplored. We are reminded once more of Europe's and Asia's response when the U.S., through the United Nations, held the line in Korea. Then, our sharpest critics (including some in India who had found us rigidly anti-Communist and obsessed with the military threat) applauded the successful deployment of American power, particularly until the fateful crossing of the 38th parallel. More recently, following Soviet and American mutual reductions of certain armaments, neutral countries who had urged this course floated inquiries about arms purchases at bargain rates.

Even assuming the present crises are partly but not exclusively military in nature, we must still face other problems. Three errors are commonly made in appraising the military component of foreign policy. First, military power is often confused with national power, and a nation's capacity to impose its will is equated with its military establishment. In reality, military power is like the fist whose force depends on the health and vitality of the body politic and the strength of the whole society. Standing armies are an important determinant of a successful foreign policy, but without other factors they will not suffice. Second, the military element is often viewed as though it depended on given factors of military strength not subject to change. The democracies in two world wars, while they have been the last to arm, have rallied their forces to gain victory in the end. Third, it is difficult to analyze and foresee the most effective distribution of the components of military force. For example, what comprises a strong military force today? Is it large ground forces, hydrogen bombs, or intensive research? Is a small, highly specialized army more desirable than a large number of ground forces, or are both essential for a nation that seeks to be strong?

The answer to these questions will probably be decisive in determining future influence in the world of states; yet it is sobering that estimates must be made on the basis of contingencies that cannot be foreseen. We know in a general way that an effective foreign policy must be supported by a military program which can safeguard national security. But this leaves those who make decisions with the painful task of allocating resources to various means of defense without any certainty of the kind of war that may have to be fought.

For more than a century and a half national security has been primarily the concern of soldiers and statesmen. In regard to postwar U.S. foreign policy, however, the American people have engaged in a succession of great debates about military strategy. Collective security, support of NATO, and nuclear weapons policy appear on the agenda of successive public discussions. There has grown up a consensus that foreign policy divorced from strength is likely to be impotent. Following two world wars, the United States dismantled its military establishment as earnest evidence of its peaceful intentions and good will. In both cases, aggressive forces bent on expansion saw such acts as an inducement to press forward; and both Germany and the Soviet Union imposed their will upon helpless nations that fell within their zone of control. Belgium in World War I and the Baltic states in World War II succumbed not because they were lacking in morality but because they found no means of securing their national frontiers. In these instances western leaders learned the hard way that weakness could be no substitute for security and that policies harnessed to power were more likely to succeed than those drawing strength from high ideals and noble expectations alone.

The United States has carried this discovery into the atomic and thermonuclear age. It is possible to argue that such peace as we have known since 1945 is the outcome of a balance of terror. There are signs that the Soviet Union has more than once marched up to the brink of war, threatening to engulf Greece and Turkey, Iran and Berlin, only to march down again when it met resistance. Conversely, where resistance proved ambiguous, uncertain, or divided—as in Egypt, Syria, and the Far East—the spread of the Soviet sphere of influence has flowed across boundaries that long marked the limits of Russian power. However, the scene and tactics of Russian imperialism have shifted. Subversion, infiltration, and indirect aggression (disguised as appeals to anti-colonialism, anti-interventionism, and anti-westernism) have put the West on the defensive on its weakest front. The Soviet Union has plowed billions of dollars into technical assistance in the developing countries. Ultimate weapons in these areas are bound to have ambiguous effects, since their use against great numbers of agrarian peoples spread over vast areas seems doubtful at best. Crises that have passed without deployment of such weapons in Vietnam, Korea, and Egypt serve to reinforce such doubts. And because the newer nations neither possess nor see the relevance of these terrible weapons, they have led the movement for their outlawry.

The Soviet military threat cannot be measured and appraised by a barometer of the rise and fall of Stalinism in the Soviet Union. If Stalinism means a brutal and heedless sacrifice of every goal to the goals of the Communist society, Stalinism lives as much today as ever. However, the fact is that Stalin no less than his successors pursued Russian objectives along more than one front even though the accent on economic-political warfare seems recently to have increased. It is undeniably true that the Russian military threat survived the death of Stalin; and if anyone has any doubt, he need only look to the sputniks, to the stress on force, and to the hundreds of Russian divisions guarding Soviet frontiers. Or he can listen to the threats and counterthreats of Russian tyrants brandishing the instruments of force at each emerging crisis, e.g., the Suez crisis, the Hungarian revolt, the Polish revolt, the Turkish-Syrian and Cuban disputes. But the countless moves and countermoves on the political and economic fronts are equally real; and with Soviet tactics of advance and retreat, the contest shifts almost imperceptibly from one type of warfare to another or sometimes is joined simultaneously on all sides. The greatest risk an observer can run is to exclude one or the other dimension of the crisis in his zeal to describe reality in shades of black and white.

To cope with the Soviet threat, the United States, which scarcely had a peacetime military policy before World War II, rapidly grouped the resources and people essential to military defense. Soon its military commitments in defense of freedom spanned the globe. In 1947, in the Rio Treaty, it joined twenty Latin American states which pledged to come to the aid of any signatory requesting help against aggression. In April, 1949, fifteen states established the North Atlantic Treaty Organization promising to regard an attack on one as an attack on all. They include Belgium, Canada, Denmark, France, West Germany, Greece, Iceland, Italy, Luxembourg, the Netherlands, Norway, Portugal, Turkey, the United Kingdom, and the United States. In September, 1951, Australia and New Zealand joined the United States in the Anzus Treaty "to meet the common danger" in the Pacific. Three years later, the Southeast Asian Treaty Organization was formed at Manila for the protection of the "general area of Southeast Asia and the Western Pacific." In case of aggression, its members (Australia, France, New Zealand, Pakistan, the Philippines, Thailand, the United Kingdom, and the United States) were to "consult immediately in order to agree to measures which should be taken for common defense." Finally, the Central Treaty Organization was formed in August, 1959, comprised of Iran, Pakistan, Turkey, and the United Kingdom; the United States, though not directly a member, undertook to cooperate in neutral defense. In addition to its multilateral commitments, the United States has bilateral agreements with more than forty states including the Philippines, Japan, Korea, and the Republic of China—in all, a vast network of connections covering the globe. To honor its undertakings, it has military bases scattered throughout the world.

In the decade and a half from July 1, 1945, to June 30, 1960, the United States provided $27,105,700,000 in military support and military assistance to allies and friendly countries. Nearly fifteen billion—the exact amount we spend annually for support of research and development in the sciences—found its way to Europe for missile aircraft, tanks, ships, motor vehicles, and electronic communications equipment. Military aid to the Near East and South Asia totaled nearly $4,500,000,000; Latin America got $389,800,000; Africa, $57,200,000; and the Far East, nearly $7,000,000,000. Beginning in 1961, a major reappraisal of foreign spending was undertaken which placed greater emphasis on aid geared to counterinsurgency and guerrilla warfare and concentrated aid in countries such as Vietnam and Laos. The United States established what amounted to an expeditionary force in South Vietnam with all the command links, support unit, and facilities associated with an overseas army. In the beginning it was a force without "fighting men" in which more than 25,000 Americans served as advisors, in support units, and as specialists. Increasingly, the United States became more deeply involved in supplying combat forces, and the number grew to 200,000. The cost of the struggle mounted to more than a million dollars a day. The former ambassador to South Vietnam, General Maxwell Taylor, argued in his book *The Uncertain Trumpet* that military policy in the 1950's placed the main but not sole reliance upon nuclear weapons. In the 1960's he pleaded for a major but not sole reliance on conventional weapons. President Kennedy took seriously his views and those of other like-minded advisors, and the war in South Vietnam has demonstrated the prophetic quality of the appraisal. From 1950 to 1954 the United States gave approximately

$2,600,000,000 to France for the war in Indochina. Since 1954 we have added substantially more than $3,000,000,000 in direct aid, and the costs are still mounting. The price of responsibility and freedom comes high in the modern world.

When confronted with expenditures of such magnitude, the average citizen is often dismayed. He would do well to remind himself that the freedom of Europe, the Near East, and areas bordering Communist China has been maintained. It is difficult to prove that these areas would have been overrun without American military assistance, for who can fathom the true intentions of Communist strategists? Nevertheless, whoever writes the scenario must record the fact that for nearly two decades no European state has lost its independence nor fallen prey to the threat of the Red Army. Communism has not added appreciably to its wartime and early postwar gains in Eastern Europe or Asia, and the factor of American military policy must clearly be counted in the balance. The annual budget for military defense has approached $50 billion, and a million men are serving their country's interests abroad. In a relatively few years the United States has developed a national security policy of major proportions, which any aggressor must take into account.

THE UNSOLVED PROBLEM OF NUCLEAR WAR

No problem facing world leaders tests political intelligence and moral imagination more severely than the issue of nuclear weapons. The awesome question of what a viable armaments policy is, is as perplexing in 1965 as it was in 1945. What are responsible governments to do with instruments of destruction? What programs can international institutions devise that will broaden the narrow spectrum of security that nations have enjoyed since World War II? Who is prepared to gamble on another's restraint with the growing stockpiles of ever more deadly weapons that nations possess? If there is no security in national weakness, can states find safety in national strength? What has happened to the criteria of national power when a few thermonuclear devices can wipe out whole populations, armies, and industrial potentials? How is the moralist to find his way between the shoals of a heedless compassion that asks too much of collective virtue and a harsh cynicism that denies the prospect of national suicide and mutual annihilation? Where do justice and security converge, and how can they be kept in balance when technology continually alters crucial elements in the equation?

To approach the armaments problem by means of a set of baffling questions is hardly reassuring, for no other realm of international relationships more desperately requires clear-cut answers and solutions. We reassure one another that reasonable men can find a way out of the present impasse if they will but contrive more imaginative policies. Those who admit stalemate or protracted uncertainty in political, economic, moral, or social conflicts instinctively prefer more precise designs and overall blueprints for the armaments problem. For example, many who see no abatement in political tensions between Moscow and Washington affirm that one action or another will assure an early end to the arms race, for failing this all men will perish. Disarmament commends itself as a sensible way out when the problems of Berlin, Formosa, or Cuba prove insoluble. To this approach the public lends assent up to the point at which policymakers carry new programs into the international arena. Then if their efforts fail, we look to explanations that question their good will, motivation, or intelligence, but rarely the stubborn quality of the problem itself. Nearly twenty years of disappointment and frustration in negotiating an end to the arms race are apparently inconclusive for the vast majority of dedicated observers.

Yet if men like George Marshall and Winston Churchill had been trusted, we could have devoted greater energy and attention to preparing to live a generation or more with the terrifying risks of nuclear destruction. It must be recalled that a handful of wise leaders feared that demands for an end to armed tension would show little sign of realization without a more basic shift in the international climate. Believing this, their prescription required more intellectual and moral effort than moralists or cynics are prone to accept. The notion that "states arm to parley" is at one and the same time offensive to pacifism and extreme militarism —two viewpoints that are often convincing and satisfying to broad sectors of public opinion.

Furthermore, when any problem as intractable as the armaments problem resists every attempt at solution, more radical approaches take the field. If warfare persists, men seek to outlaw it. When great power negotiations break down, the public at large demands that "people speak to people." An unquenchable faith in reason, by which modern civilization has advanced, generates the belief that no issue which divides men can long remain outside the boundaries of genuine understanding. Failure to solve a problem therefore leads to a search for a scapegoat, whether imperfect institutions, ill-prepared negotiators, or laggard policy-makers. Someone must have been asleep at the switch, for otherwise reason and humanity would surely have freed us from the dread crisis.

Any analysis which stresses elements of the armaments problem that heretofore have not been solved by serious and responsible leaders is bound to evoke hostility and deep distrust. Critics will ask if the observer intends to leave millions of helpless men and women to their fate. They will wish to know what has happened to his sense of moral revulsion to war, to a renunciation of the acts and means of violence, or to the compelling lesson that man should love, not seek to destroy, his brother? Moreover, they will wonder whether the student of international conflict does not move unconsciously and imperceptibly from describing the facts of international life as he sees them to a posture of belaboring those who condemn him for his callousness and immorality? Then, too, the student runs the further risk of developing a vested interest in the status quo, with all its tragic failures and shattered hopes. The more he observes the cancerous state of affairs brought about by such profound divisions as the rift between East and West, the more he will come to accept it,

at least in the short run, and, barring fundamental changes, view
it as a permanent condition to be relieved, temporarily alleviated,
but never—from his angle of vision—fully eliminated or cured.
This is the occupational hazard of those who shape armaments
policies.

Yet the moral risks of facing reality will not excuse the diplomatist any more that the doctor from accepting the distressing
burdens that are inherent in his task. If all patients were free
of disease at all times, the doctor's place could appropriately
be filled by someone else with other training and skills. If the
international stage were not plagued by rivalry, distrust, and
suspicion, negotiators who have learned to take conflict in stride
would quickly become obsolete. Incidentally, no diplomatist
worthy of the name believes that warfare is inevitable. It is conflict and rivalry, particularly among those who contend for
influence and authority, that are taken for granted; and the search
for ways and means to limit rivalries and prevent the struggle
for power from crossing over into open strife and war is un-
remitting.

The vocation and the commitment of the negotiator compel
him to believe that war is not inevitable. When the inflammation
caused by tension and rivalry grows too intense, he must apply
a poultice to relieve the infection until time and circumstances
can restore health to the body politic. If he were to act as if the
infection were imaginary or could be "reasoned" away, he would
fail in his calling, however humane and civilized his motives
might be. The doctor can hardly assume that health will supplant
disease once and for all; neither can the diplomat proceed as if
virtue were obliterating sinfulness or cooperation had superseded
conflict.

For some with sensitive consciences the need to recognize the
dual existence of good and evil can be profoundly distressing.
Few liberals or humanists deny the reality of imperfect virtue;
and they labor faithfully to reduce, not eliminate, human suffering through social reform and aid to the oppressed. They
accept the necessity of charity, even within blatantly oppressive

and unjust social systems whose purposes they must ultimately condemn. Here liberals and, particularly, pacifists link the "incompatible" forces of an ethic of love and coexistence with tyrannical regimes. Thus, programs of aid have been organized by the Friends in South Africa and certain Communist countries.

Because I believe they are right in striving to bring aid and comfort to victims of an unjust political order, even at the risk of strengthening that order, I am puzzled by their austere rejection of ethical pragmatism in confronting the armaments problem. Surely limited war is morally preferable to total war, and the cold war is to be preferred to a shooting war. Yet moral relativists who see some justice in the most tyrannical regimes become moral absolutists in the claim that there is "no other course but the final rejection of war as an instrument for achieving justice." I would not ask men to form an unholy alliance with evil nor justify what is wrong, but I would hope they might reflect and conclude that cooperation with evil in the interests of good cannot be defended in political and social relations and utterly condemned in the international and military realm.

I suspect the source of this illusion rests in the belief that men can draw an absolute distinction between strategies of violence and nonviolence. Nonviolent resistance is often equated with the pure gospel of love. Sometimes indeed, it may be morally superior to violence. However, Western Judaeo-Christian ethics has nothing to say about the absolute moral superiority of stratagems of nonviolence through which one group seeks to impose its will on another. The seeds of evil in human relations, including politics, cluster around a man's desire and necessity, as he sees it, to have his way with someone else, restricting thereby the self-fulfillment of human personality. The basis of wrongdoing would seem to be the encroachment of one will on another and the denial of self-realization and individuality. Violence is a more egregious form of this evil, but it is not fundamentally a thing apart.

I fear moral absolutism in the face of the nuclear problem

partly because ethical resources are so desperately needed in the proximate decisions of military policy. I must agree with the statement of the British Council of Churches that "restraint is a major Christian objective." Yet, if liberal and humane men can only condemn military programs as a whole, as some have traditionally denounced all forms of politics, who will defend the objective of restraint? Who will speak for reason, self-limitation, and restricting the buildup of defenses to proportions that will deter and inhibit a reckless enemy without an endless striving to surpass him in every weapon with a vast armory of destructiveness? Who will hold the reins on policies of unconditional surrender and programs aimed at liquidating an opponent? Who will pursue the goal of limiting conflicts both in scope and character? Who will defend restraint, not escalation or withdrawal in Vietnam?

If moral certainty in the control and elimination of nuclear weapons exceeds the wit and attainment of man, no one who desires to serve his nation and the world responsibly can abandon the search for more viable solutions to limited problems. The irony of the nuclear age is that all-out war has lost its inner logic, but no major power across the vast chasm of mutual distrust can afford to be the first to found its policies upon this premise. However, the first level at which moral compulsion properly takes the stage is at the point where man's necessity to control and eliminate warfare conflicts with his inability to do so. Those who assert that the practical man must "accept war in the abstract as a fact of life" are doubtless correct, as are those who point out that most choices the statesman makes are practical ones at several stages removed from the moral issue. Yet moral man, faced with mankind's extinction, has an obligation by virtue of common humanity to resist in every practical way the unfolding of a chain of events that will lead to disaster.

Moral responsibility for others no less than for himself requires a man to act with moral and political discrimination to prevent war, to restrict its spread once it erupts, and to bring it to an end as promptly and decisively as possible. Moral discrimination is an unending process, and those who would restrict it to outlawing war and the instruments of war confine it to too narrow limits. The compulsion to seek moral distinctions across a wide spectrum of war and peace is generated by a morality comprehensive enough to embrace both means and ends. For these reasons the moralist is entitled to speak not merely about war in the abstract but about particular wars and the military and political conditions that either increase the likelihood of war or threaten to carry a struggle beyond the point of self-defense or beyond the necessities of national or international interests. We know enough about the tendencies of men and nations to assert that great weakness has almost always invited expansion and aggression by those possessing great strength. The duty of statesmen is to reduce the temptation for dynamic expansionist movements to spread their influence and their cause. At the same time, under circumstances of present-day technology, nations can ill afford to build defense systems capable alone of wars of last recourse. Despite repeated claims that conventional wars have been rendered obsolete, outbreaks since World War II have all been conventional in nature. Military conflict and the threat of conflict in Korea, Hungary, Suez, Vietnam, and Lebanon have followed the conventional pattern. Nor is the argument convincing that the West has no practical alternative. A leading military analyst writes: "Many of the assumptions regarding the impossibility of conventional defense and . . . the 'hordes' of Communist manpower, are either fallacious or exaggerated. Both in total available manpower and in its industrial potential the free world still is superior."

Neither national necessity nor military logic can excuse American diplomatic and intellectual leaders from considering principles defining the limits of military preparation and conduct. An armaments program aimed at achieving nuclear superiority must be questioned both on military and ethical grounds, for the purpose of thermonuclear strength is to confront an adversary

with the certainty of severe retaliation, sufficient to make the
adventure too costly. The goal under present-day conditions
cannot be organizing the means of victory since the real defeat
is the war itself. Yet reasonable prudence in establishing limited
nuclear strength may prove a deterrent to those who might
otherwise dare use weapons they monopolize. Even a great and
humane people may succumb to temptation, and we are constrained to speculate over what course we might have followed
at Hiroshima had others possessed the atomic bomb.

The United States cannot afford to reject cavalierly "the principle of proportion," whatever the difficulties of enforcing restraint. This ancient principle, as enunciated in the classical
writings on the just war, still holds good that grave injustices may
not be repressed by means which cause greater injustice than the
perpetuation of the original injustice. I am not convinced that
a reexamination of the classic texts on the conditions of a just
war or of a defensive war is outmoded in our time. The great
publicists of the past were more inclined than some of our latter-
day international lawyers to view law and justice in context. They
searched their souls and the practice of states to ascertain when
and how states and princes could be expected to keep their commitments. Circumstances led them to write less of enforcement
systems and more of conditions of self-interest and mutual trust.
They talked of levels and orders of justice and were not above
accepting the compromises absolute justice was compelled to
make if a tolerable order were to be preserved. Any system of
limitation must serve the national interests of all parties. We are
told that an armaments agreement will be self-enforcing if com-
pliance serves these interests better than evasion or violation.
The underpinnings of every international arrangement are, of
course, moral in character. There must be a minimum of mutual
trust. The basic problem in East-West relations has been and
remains the conspicuous absence of such trust.

If this trust is to be created, it must grow from the discovery
of mutual interests so overpowering as to transcend sharp ideo-

logical cleavages. Do Russians and Americans have a common interest in attacking the problem of wheat-borne virus? Do they share a mutual interest in restricting the spread and diffusion of atomic weapons among the smaller powers? Have they not been driven to inhibit the risk of contaminating the atmosphere by ending nuclear tests? Do they not have an equal stake in restraining buoyant and reckless powers who on ideological or political grounds would plunge the world into a deathly atomic holocaust? The truth is that answers will come as part of a slow, gradual process. History yields to human initiative, and evil may yet spawn good.

The ideas of restraint, proportionality, and limitation have a very practical bearing on armaments policy. Restraint means that nuclear weapons may not be multiplied beyond the point of serving a security function. The principle of proportionality assumes that the means employed are proportionate to the goal undertaken. For example, the United States seeks to deter Soviet military adventures through its nuclear armaments program, not assure an easy and painless total military victory. A nation whose objective is national and international security is obligated to pursue armaments programs that faithfully reflect this purpose. It can hardly engage in an unlimited buildup of weapons once the weapons lose their obvious security function. Restraint and proportionality may commend a renewed stress on conventional armaments rather than an accelerating nuclear weapons programs. They may mean that strengthening existing missile sites is more acceptable than adding to the missile stockpile. The merging of insights from England and the United States, both drawing on two thousand years of political thought and experience in Western civilization, provides an essential foundation for viewing this altogether crucial problem of the control of armaments and the limitation of the use of force.

II

PROPHETS, PRACTITIONERS,
AND THE MORAL ISSUE

*The moral life is not slavish conformity to an unrelenting
code.*   PAUL TILLICH

THE nuclear problem is illustrative of the moral and political
issues that perplex and baffle our times. Secretary of State Dean
Rusk has referred to them as "the problems that make pygmies
of us all." It would be possible to review and analyze foreign
aid or support for the United Nations and Vietnam in comparable terms. They remain unsolved problems of our foreign policy
and do not readily yield to simple solutions. If foreign relations
suffer from a chronic illness, it is the deep-seated yearning of
Americans to dispose promptly and once and for all of our most
troublesome problems. The idea of a grand design or a total
solution periodically makes inroads on national thinking. It

33

provides a release from popular frustration and fatigue but for the most part leaves problems unsolved and unchanged. Once the first flush of enthusiasm has passed, restlessness and uneasiness remain. The problems also remain encased in a hardened crust of unfulfilled expectations and unrealized aspirations.

Fortunately, a handful of extraordinarily creative and determined prophets and practitioners throw light on our predicament. Together they offer a distillation of the essence of the Anglo-American approach. It is futile to argue whether they provide the missing doctrine of foreign relations about which critics periodically speak. There are handicaps as well as advantages in dogmas and doctrines. Our best minds and most experienced leaders are helpful in providing a framework for foreign policy. If the layman or the scholar examines their thought with sympathy and imagination, he is likely to draw from their wisdom certain guidelines or general principles that will help him chart a course along an otherwise treacherous and bewildering route. These leaders contribute knowledge essential to a more rational approach to unsolved problems.

The contribution of prophets has been to unfold and illuminate the long view for a system of government that must inevitably focus attention on short-range policies. Our policy-makers are condemned to put out the fires that break out daily around the world. They do their thinking along a changing front of immediate crises and problems. There will be changes of governments each year in about one third of the approximately 120 nations with which the United States has diplomatic relations. Overt or potential conflicts threaten at every point on the globe. The fate of the Policy Planning Council in the Department of State is to spend more time on policy than on planning. It has tended to become more operational and less forward-looking. The task of viewing the future has devolved on philosophers, historians, and political thinkers. In this realm, historians like Arnold J. Toynbee, Herbert Butterfield, and Walter Millis have made the most lasting contribution.

Toynbee, by the boldness of his approach and his impressive erudition, has had most to say about the long-range prospects of contemporary western civilization. The student of his monumental *Study of History* and his other writings can identify three major stages in his philosophy of history. These changes in emphasis and in frame of reference reveal his ability to formulate a theory, discover its flaws through trial and error, and exchange it for something he considers better. They also disclose that his conception of history as a saga of civilizations and ultimately of religion is an idea that dawned on him only gradually.

Toynbee's first publications are clearly the children of his training. His education at Winchester and Balliol coincides roughly with the first decade of this century. The symbol and key to the times was the Diamond Jubilee of Queen Victoria, and as a small boy he had stood in the processions. Englishmen then shared the feeling of having reached the summit where history had been fulfilled. This philosophy can hardly have been very convincing to Toynbee, for his earlier writings reflect a concern for divers peoples and nationalities in the selfsame spirit to which President Woodrow Wilson was to appeal in his creed of national self-determination.

From 1914 to 1916 Toynbee's first essays and books were published.[1] In them his methodology is not defined in so many words but reflected in the subjects he considers. Not civilizations but nations are the "intelligible units of history." He reserves for nations in general the same optimism that the Victorian era showed for Britain in particular. In our age, he says, "the national state is the most magnificent . . . social achievement in existence."[2] National culture is sacred, and to oppose it is to

1　Arnold J. Toynbee *et al., The Balkans: A History of Bulgaria, Serbia, Greece, Rumania and Turkey* (London: Oxford University Press, 1915); Arnold J. Toynbee, *Nationality and the War* (London: J. M. Dent & Sons, 1915); Arnold J. Toynbee, *The New Europe: Some Essays in Reconstruction* (New York: E. P. Dutton & Co., 1916).

2　Toynbee, *Nationality and the War*, 481.

defy God. One recognizes inspiration from the secular aspects of Wilsonian nationalism in the fervor with which Toynbee handles his subject.

Some of the same terms and metaphors which he later uses to describe the role of religion are used to characterize the function of nation-states. For example, he finds that "within the chrysalis" of absolute government a "common self-consciousness or Nationality"[3] is born, and democratic nationalism is becoming a healthy and strapping youngster. "From the Ottoman Empire there would emerge . . . as from a chrysalis, a Turkish nation. . . ."[4] In the same way he later finds that civilizations emerge from the "chrysalis" of great religions.

These examples of a rather naïve belief in bourgeois progress through humanitarian nationalism are, of course, qualified in many ways. At an early date a profound belief in some form of international authority is in evidence. Eastern Europe has problems which require a Balkan Zollverein. Culture is not inherent in any one language but is the heritage of the race. But these foreshadowings of later "universalism" are more the expressions of an idealistic philosophy of international relations than a denial of the primacy of nations as units of history. Indeed, his belief that World War I was a kind of accident which but temporarily disturbed Europe's progress toward a warless internationalism is concrete evidence that at this stage in Toynbee's thinking idealism and nationalism are indissolubly wedded. The European national state is the norm of civilized society and has so far revealed a "faculty of indefinite organic growth."[5] A premonition that this perspective may change, however, comes in the last sentence of *Nationality and War*. If nations continue cribbed and confined within parochial states in their struggles

3 *Ibid.*, 273.
4 Arnold J. Toynbee and Kenneth P. Kirkwood, *Turkey* (London: Ernest Benn, 1926), 4–5.
5 Toynbee *et al.*, *The Balkans*, 183.

for existence and survival, Toynbee says, their fate may prove to be no different than that of the Greek city-states. This was the kind of history he wrote as a young man of twenty-five.

This early outlook was shattered by World War I. Any bourgeois illusions about human progress could scarcely have withstood so grim a parable of man's violence and brutality. For five years Toynbee immersed himself in propaganda and intelligence work for the government. His assignment was to sift and rewrite reports of German atrocities. These lurid accounts flow incongruously from the pen of the judicious historian. After the war he observed, "Atrocities seem to be outbreaks of bestiality normally 'suppressed' in human beings but almost automatically stimulated under certain conditions, and that so powerfully, if the conditions are sufficiently acute or protracted, that the most highly civilized people are carried away."[6] Moreover, he registered serious misgivings concerning the nation-state as the measure of things. No known civilization except Western civilization has grounded statehood on community of language. This formula has occasioned bloodshed and massacre in the Near East and Middle East. To paraphrase Toynbee: it has climaxed in a totalitarian Moloch, in a demoniac effort after uniformity.

A second impression penetrated Toynbee's consciousness during this crisis. In the spring of 1918, as the German offensive under Ludendorff exploded in one final thrust, a profound anxiety hung over his thought. During 1911–12, immediately after taking his degree, he had made a nine months' walking trip through Greece and Crete. One impression engraved itself indelibly on his memory. In the faint shadows of the Minoan civilization in Crete, he came upon the deserted country house of a Venetian landowner. As he looked at these ruins of two and a half centuries, he imagined those of Britain heaped along-

6 Arnold J. Toynbee, *The Western Question in Greece and Turkey: A Study in the Contact of Civilisations* (London: Constable & Co., 1922), 266.

side them. In 1918 he recalled this *memento mori* of an extinct
Venetian colony in Crete, which had lasted four and a half
centuries longer than any British colony. The ominous prospect
that the German drive might prove the "knock-out blow" for
the West impelled Toynbee to reread Thucydides and Lucretius,
including the latter's imperishable, if melancholy, counsel on
how to face death. These somber accounts of Peloponnesian and
Hannibalic doom, the fierce and brutal catastrophes which Toynbee himself was reading about and narrating, and his impending
sense of the ephemeral nature of civilization swelled to an ob-
session following his trip to the Balkans. They were the three
elements destined to be blended into an alloy of suitable tem-
per and resiliency to provide Toynbee with a new vessel of
history.

The second stage or period in Toynbee's historical method
began in 1922, when at the age of thirty-three he drafted on half
a sheet of paper the main outlines of *A Study of History*. It was
to be a work twice the size of Gibbon's great classic; and on it,
as we now know, Toynbee mortgaged most of his intellectual
strength and vigor. During the war years forces were carrying
him toward a perspective which embraced and enriched the
whole historical landscape. This was made clear when in 1919
he addressed the candidates for *literae humaniores* at Oxford
following his first year of postwar teaching at the University of
London. The thesis of the lecture is a concise paradigm of his
new theory of history. Gone is the nation-state as the primary
unit of study, for "the plot of civilisation in a great exposition
of it—like the Hellenic exposition of our own Western exposition—is surely the right goal of a humane education."[7] Western
society, he asserts somewhat later, is "a closer and more permanent unity than . . . the independent states that form and dissolve

7   Arnold J. Toynbee, *The Tragedy of Greece: A Lecture De-
livered for the Professor of Greek to Candidates for Honours
in Literae Humaniores at Oxford in May 1920* (London: Oxford University Press, 1931), 6.

within its boundaries. . . ."[8] Having substituted civilizations for nations, Toynbee is ready with a second innovation. How are these great units to be analyzed and dissected? His answer is the same as that given by Oswald Spengler, though the latter's writings were not yet known to Toynbee. The life histories of civilizations must be compiled, compared, and generalized in a "morphology" of history. It can be observed that civilizations pass through determinate states of growth and decay. For the purpose of describing these stages, civilizations can be considered as "biological organisms." In this limited sense one can speak precisely about the life cycles of societies as living creatures.

In the same way, Toynbee casts the life patterns of his civilizations in the form of a second metaphor—that of a drama or tragedy. He plainly expects that "the great civilizations . . . may all reveal the same plot, if we analyze them rightly." It is this plot and its three "acts"—growth and development; crisis, breakdown, and rally; final dissolution—which the universal historian must gird himself to study. The Graeco-Roman civilization is Toynbee's model, and he develops his own thesis to account for its decline. For him, the moment of moral failure and breakdown came in 431 B.C. with the Peloponnesian War.

A third and final technique should be mentioned. After choosing civilizations as his subject and breaking down their histories into three parts or "acts" of a drama, Toynbee poses a third methodological problem concerning the relationships between these units. There are issues in history that would be lost from sight if one examined merely the uniqueness or, as with Spengler, the "culture-soul" of each separate civilization. So for Toynbee the most absorbing problem in history is that of the encounters or contacts in which new civilizations are born.

The present encounter between Western civilization and the rest of the world is not something novel or unique. It is rather

8   Arnold J. Toynbee, *The Western Question in Greece and Turkey: A Study in the Contact of Civilisations* (2nd ed.; London: Constable & Co., 1923), 4.

an outstanding instance of a recurrent historical phenomenon which can be examined in comparative terms. From the study of encounters between historic civilizations, "laws" can be deduced regarding cultural contacts. One "law" which Toynbee tries out focuses on the nature of relationships in the face of resistance by an assaulted society. A civilization is ordinarily not susceptible to the total culture of a foreign society. When two civilizations collide, the culture of the more aggressive one is diffracted into its components, just as a light ray is refracted into a spectrum by a prism. The more trivial components which will not cause too immediate and violent a disturbance of the threatened society's traditional way of life have the best chance of penetration. Illustrative are two successive assaults of Western civilization upon China and Japan. The Far East, which in the sixteenth and seventeenth centuries had repulsed an attempt to introduce the Western way of life en bloc—including its religion, yielded in the nineteenth century to the more trivial force of technology. It was able at least to accept this while retaining the more basic qualities of its own way of life.

This diffraction of culture leads to another recurrent feature of encounters between civilizations. An institution or social phenomenon that is an organic part of a total culture may, when separated from the whole in the form of a culture-ray, threaten or undermine the assaulted society. Thus the nation-state, when founded on common linguistic groups, as in Western Europe, has been relatively unexplosive. Outside this geographic area, in Eastern Europe, Southwest Asia, India, and Malaya, where the linguistic map has not always provided a convenient or logical basis for the political map, the nation-state has been a disruptive force. From the Sudetanland to Eastern Europe, nations have been established by methods of barbarism, war and expansionism, because the historic and traditional local patterns of social life in the areas clashed with the imperative of national self-determination. The original setting of modern nationalism, in which linguistic groups were compact and homogeneous units, has frequently been missing in non-European societies; and the idea of nationalism therefore has become an unsettling, even volcanic, force.[9]

It must be evident that Toynbee's *modus operandi* in dealing with history has undergone radical transformations since 1914–15. The most decisive change of all, however, took place in 1939 and ushered in the third period of his historical method. At the age of fifty, Toynbee shifted the pivot of his approach from "civilisations" to "higher religions." Hitherto religion had been a means to an end, an agent responsible for the reproduction and perpetuation of civilizations. In the second batch of volumes of *A Study of History*, twice published in sets of three, an unexpected note is sounded as a distinct counterbeat to these earlier views. In volume V he explains:

> When we examine the universal churches we shall find ourselves led to raise the question whether churches can really be comprehended in their entirety in the framework of the histories of civilizations, within which they make their first historical appearance, or whether we have not to regard them as representatives of another species of society which is at least as distinct from the species "civilisations" as the civilisations are distinct from the primitive societies.
>
> This may prove to be one of the most momentous questions that a study of history . . . can suggest to us. . . .[10]

The change is bound up with the pattern of disintegration, which is manifested in the later stages of all civilizations. The whole apparatus of disintegration with internal and external proletariats or forces of rebellion within or outside the civilization as well as religion is a key element in Toynbee's conception of the pattern of history. Our interest here, however, is restricted to the one suggestion that in a curious but perceptible fashion Toynbee has moved from "nations" to "civilisations" to "higher

9 Toynbee deals with these questions in the last four volumes of *A Study of History* (12 vols.; London: Oxford University Press, 1934—).

10 Toynbee, *A Study of History*, V, 23.

religions" and that these shifts in historical focus have altered profoundly both his interpretation and the tools and techniques he employs. He has summarized this change and its consequences in words that leave little doubt as to this most recent perspective:

> Our present view of modern history focuses attention on the rise of our modern Western secular civilisation as the latest great new event in the world. As we follow that rise, from the first premonition of it in the genius of Frederick II Hohenstaufen, through the Renaissance to the eruption of democracy and science and modern scientific technique, we think of all this as being the great new event in the world which demands our attention and commands our admiration. If we can bring ourselves to think of it, instead, as one of the vain repetitions of the Gentiles—an almost meaningless repetition of something that the Greeks and Romans did before us and did supremely well—then the greatest new event in the history of mankind will be seen to be a very different one. The greatest new event will then not be the monotonous rise of yet another secular civilisation out of the bosom of the Christian Church in the course of these latter centuries; it will still be the Crucifixion and its spiritual consequences.[11]

When he reaches the point of appraising the future of Western civilization, Toynbee tends to suspend judgment. There are for Toynbee three possibilities, and in measuring them he reveals a position of great reserve and caution. In a letter to me of April 19, 1950, he explains: "I am, as you know not a determinist, so I certainly think that my work cannot be used for making definite predictions. Insofar as Spengler's can, I feel that is a weakness in his work." A first possible destiny as he sees it is that western civilization will suffer a great and unparalleled catastrophe. What makes this prospect so real and so terrifying is the level of our attainments in harnessing forces of nature and our accompanying failure to achieve a comparable mastery over human nature. If the first possibility should be realized, not only our civilization but quite possibly the whole human race would

11   Arnold J. Toynbee, *Civilisation on Trial* (New York: Oxford University Press, 1948), 237.

be destroyed. He envisages the loss of all that mankind has gained in the last six thousand years. A second contingency is the preservation of civilization at a price he considers prohibitive. A universal state might usher in total regimentation and control. The means could be found to abolish famine and war, but in the process inhabitants of a "brave new world" might bargain away freedom and human dignity. A third possibility would be the discovery of a middle way between total destruction and absolute regimentation. Following this route, mankind might rescue society from war and tyranny while assuring it of continually renewed energy and vitality for future tasks and challenges. Thus, for Toynbee, the future remains an open question.

In nobility of purpose, Woodrow Wilson towers above the prophets whose voices have sounded on this side of the Atlantic. His vision of a world of free and democratic states still remains a goal for the future. His prophecy failed, for he assumed that "national purposes have fallen more and more into the background and the common purpose of enlightened mankind has taken their place."[12] His early hope that international society would prosper if governments based on national self-determination emerged following World War I collided with the need for larger economic groupings, especially in the Balkans. He was too ready to conclude that American principles and policies are "also the principles and policies of forward-looking men and women everywhere, of every modern nation, of every enlightened community. They are the principles of mankind and must prevail."[13] Yet by his towering idealism he held out hope for a warring international society in search of a new and better world. Unfortunately, his plans were rejected, not only abroad by cyn-

12   Woodrow Wilson, Fourth Liberty Loan Address, September 27, 1918.
13   Woodrow Wilson, *The New Democracy: Presidential Messages, Addresses, and Other Papers (1915–17)*, ed. Ray Standard Baker and William E. Dodd (2 vols., New York: Harper and Brothers, 1926), II, 414.

ical and skillful diplomatists but at home by a people not prepared for a League of Nations and a partnership to enforce peace. His prophecy lived on and helped to inspire the architects of the United Nations.

There is another more scholarly Wilson whose views are largely obscured by the memory of his visions as a tragic political leader. He understood as a political scientist that "society is not a crowd, but an organism; and, like every organism, it must grow as a whole. . . . This organic whole, Society . . . must grow by the development of its aptitudes and desires. . . . The evolution of its institutions must take place by slow modification and nice all-round adjustment. And all this is but a careful and abstract way of saying that no reform may succeed for which the major thought of the nation is not prepared. . . ."[14] The leader must serve the slow-paced daily need of the people. "In no case may we safely hurry the organism away from its habit: for it is held together by that habit."[15] The leader must discern and strengthen the tendencies that make for development. Practical leadership "must daily feel the road that leads to the goal proposed, knowing that it is a slow, a very slow, evolution. . . . Society must walk, dependent upon practicable paths, incapable of scaling sudden, precipitous heights, a roadbreaker, not a fowl of the air."[16] Wilson was prepared to accept the dictum of Edmund Burke that the leader's task is "to follow, not to force the public inclination, to give a direction, a form, a technical dress, and a specific sanction, to the general sense of community. That general sense of the community may wait to be aroused, and the statesman must arouse it; may be inchoate and vague, and the statesman must formulate it and make it

14   Wood Wilson, *Leaders of Men* (Princeton: Princeton University Press, 1952), 41.
15   *Ibid.*, 43.
16   *Ibid.*, 44–45.

explicit."[17] The young Wilson was persuaded that the leader could not, and should not, do more. "The forces of the public thought may be blind; he must lend them sight; they may blunder: he must set them right."[18] But his creation is one of form, not substance; and without popular force behind him, he can do nothing. He sows his grain in season, nurturing and bringing it to harvest.

How ironic that someone so acutely aware of the limits of leadership should end his days a failure. And yet, in the longer view, his failure was temporary, his prophecy enduring. The literary and prophetic mind as Wilson saw it "conceives images . . . unlimited, unvaried by accident."[19] The prophet is guided less by principles, as statesmen conceive them, than by concepts and the long-range outlook. Principles for the statesman are threads running through the labyrinth of circumstances. As the prophet views them they are unities. In placing Wilson in the stream of Anglo-American thought, the student can do no better than to recite his own distinction: "Throw the conceiving mind, habituated to contemplating wholes, into the arena of politics, and it seems to itself to be standing upon shifting sands, where no sure foothold, and no upright posture are possible. Its ideals are to it more real and solid than any actuality of the world in which men are managed."[20]

The heirs of the Wilsonian tradition share much of his fervor and dedication to universalism. Ironically, a leader best remembered for his skill as a negotiator and his strong words on brinkmanship and massive retaliation held to the same prophetic faith. Thus, John Foster Dulles could write: "The broad principles that should govern our international conduct are not obscure. They grow out of the practice by the nations of the simple things Christ taught. . . . Such principles mark the channels into which

17   *Ibid.*, 45.
18   *Ibid.*
19   *Ibid.*, 46.
20   *Ibid.*

our minds must direct our international acts if they are to be productive of permanent good."[21]

Dulles saw these principles as requiring for nations no less than individual self-sacrifice in the interest of universal human welfare. He called for a mood of genuine repentance by individuals and corporate societies alike. Possession of natural resources was a trust to be discharged in the general interest. The United States "must be ready to subordinate immediate and particular national interests to the welfare of all."[22] It was possible to envisage for the state the same quality of material unselfishness that religion cherished for the individual. An international federation for peace which would include all states was to be the beginning of a world government. Even the world's greatest naval and air power, the United States, must accept the truth that "the right to close the world's highways will never conduce to permanent peace unless it resides in a body deriving its authority from a consent that is broadly international in scope."[23] And in reviewing concrete foreign policies, Dulles affirmed that foreign aid ought to be "given out of compassion or because of love of our fellow man . . . [not] in order to achieve certain political objectives."[24] Through the war years and after, he stressed the importance of the General Assembly of the United Nations as the site for moral judgments that would translate the universal moral law into policy. Indeed the moral law as reflected in the moral consensus of mankind was an autonomous force and the best sanction for world law.

The most noteworthy contrast between Wilson and Dulles is

---

21 John Foster Dulles, "The American People Need Now to Be Imbued with a Righteous Faith," in *A Righteous Faith for a Just and Durable Peace* (New York: The Commission to Study the Basis of a Just and Durable Peace, 1942), 10.

22 *Ibid.*, 103–104. (E. R. Platig's writings on Dulles are the basis of my interpretation.)

23 John Foster Dulles, article in *Fortune*, XXV (January, 1942), 88.

24 New York *Times*, April 15, 1952, p. 2.

the gradual dilution of the latter's universalism in the face of circumstances. While Wilson became less pragmatic and more idealistic as the nation's chief executive, Dulles' intellectual journey was precisely the opposite. Historians have pointed out that Dulles throughout his career played successive roles first as a highly successful lawyer, then as the Protestant church's foremost spokesman on international relations in the Federal and the National Council of Churches, and finally as the nation's chief minister of foreign policy. He appears most consistently as the legal advocate charged with making his client's case clear and effective. In 1913, as Wilson moved into the White House, Dulles was beginning a highly successful legal career. In 1919 he became a member of the important "steering committee" of the American delegation at the Paris Peace Conference. He carried the major burden of American representation on the Committee on Reparations Clauses in the treaties with Austria, Hungary, and Bulgaria. He argued that Germany should pay reparations for damages but not bear all the costs of the war, as the French and British insisted. While Germany's war-making was morally reprehensible, he maintained that "it is not enough that an act be immoral . . . unless at the same time it is illegal." Germany should accept liability for war costs in theory but pay reparations only for damages—a principle that formed the basis for the famous "war guilt clause" of the Treaty of Versailles.

The Oxford Conference (1937) was the turning point in Dulles' approach to international morality. In his early career he had drawn a rather sharp distinction between the ethical and the political. He distinguished between the norm of how man should act and the facts of political behavior. In commenting on the reports of the Oxford Conference, he warned that spiritual leaders ought not to engage in "advocacy of particular political solutions . . ., for specific measures will almost always involve matters of close judgment and of expediency and will seldom be such an embodiment of Christ's teachings that the Church can permit the two to be equated." At this stage he came close to asserting that the normative theory of the church was not directly applicable to real life problems. He warned of the "pitfalls which the worldly constantly prepare for those who secure for themselves the appearance of the church's benediction." Indeed there are national heroes who "particularly conduce to war. One is the crusading hero who champions the cause of [national] justice." In a paper prepared in 1948 for the World Council of Churches Dulles declared: "The writer is, indeed, one who believes that the Church ought not to make authoritative pronouncements with respect to detailed action in political, economic or social fields. Practical political action is not often a subject for authoritative moral judgments of universal scope."

The startling contrast between the reasoned pragmatism of this approach and Dulles' crusading idealism suggests that he was wont to distinguish between analysis and action. He believed that absolute idealism engendered moral response and the political leader had obligations denied to the spiritual leader. Churchmen must take into account "what men are, not what the Church thinks they ought to be." In 1949 he placed in the *Congressional Record* a statement commending our policy for having joined "at Yalta . . . with the Soviet Union and the United Kingdom in pledging to assist the liberated nations of Europe and the Axis satellite states alike to create democratic institutions of their own choice."[25] By the 1952 campaign, however, he condemned Yalta as a "sell-out." If there is hypocrisy in this, it resides in his belief that ideals "permit us to measure our progress" but are not imperatives at any given moment for practical action. Men in politics act from selfish motives; men reformed act in accordance with rational self-sacrifice in behalf of the highest good. They are moved to action by moralistic appeals to idealism, and this is best achieved through the public utterances of righteous political leaders.

The role of Reinhold Niebuhr has been one of bridging the

25 *Congressional Record*, 81st Cong., 1st Sess., XCV, Pt. 9, p. 12532.

wide gulf between moralism and pragmatism. In a virtual torrent of books and essays, Niebuhr has struggled to reconcile ethics and politics. For scholars and intellectuals, his accomplishments are more satisfying than the writings and speeches of the prophets. Indeed he sometimes appears suspended between prophet and practitioner. He is persuaded that only a handful of cynics dismiss the moral issue. A much larger group falls prey to the perils of hypocrisy, which claims more for the moral quality of an act than the facts warrant. Men in international affairs honestly seek to achieve righteousness, but they cloak their selfish acts in the guise of moral perfectionism. He has been a frequent critic of a form of self-righteousness he associated with Secretary Dulles. He complained that Dulles in speaking to a convention of the National Council of Churches at Cleveland in the fall of 1958 was the captive of a moral universe that "made everything quite clear, too clear, with the result that it complicated our relations with our allies, who found our self-righteousness very vexatious. For self-righteousness is the inevitable fruit of simple moral judgments, placed in the service of moral complacency."[26] He quotes Dulles as saying that "the Communists deny there is such a thing as justice, in our meaning of the term" and asks what is meant by the pronoun "our." Justice, according to Aristotle, means giving each man his due. In politics it is always a balancing of objective standards and a tolerable equilibrium of social forces. Niebuhr questions whether China's policy toward the offshore islands is wholly a product of their standards of justice. "If China were not communist, it would still have a different perspective from ours on that strategic problem and might still object to our insistence that the Formosan Government is the real government of China."[27] Niebuhr singles out another proposition in Dulles' lecturing to our allies on the basis of the "principle" of action. Dulles had complained that

26 Reinhold Niebuhr, "The Moral World of Foster Dulles," *New Republic*, CXXXIX (December 1, 1958), 8.
27 *Ibid.*

"our collective security arrangements would surely collapse if our free world associates felt that they were tied to policies that shifted under the dictates of passing considerations, as to what was expedient from the standpoint of the United States. They do not like it when we adhere to principle, but they would like it even less, if we had no principles." To this Niebuhr replies that "Mr. Dulles forgot that what our allies like least of all is our tendency to equate our inflexibility with 'principle,' and their more flexible policy with 'expediency.' "[28]

Niebuhr is fond of quoting the words of the late Justice Oliver Wendell Holmes: "People are always extolling the man of principles; but I think the superior man is the one who knows that he must find his way in a maze of principles." In an equally telling phrase, Niebuhr observes: "The fact that honest men see the hierarchy of moral values and principles in a different order according to their different perspectives must not discourage us from honestly seeking to do what is right. But it ought to dissuade us from all self-righteous assumptions that we alone are truly moral."[29] He has not reserved his strictures for American leaders. When India defied the United Nations' order for a plebiscite in predominantly Moslem Kashmir, Nehru took the law into his hands. He could not risk a plebiscite which almost certainly would have gone against India; and so he swiftly annexed the larger part of Kashmir, which had already been integrated into the Indian economy. For Niebuhr, Nehru's conduct merely proved Goethe's shrewd observation that "conscience is the virtue of observers and not of agents of action." "When India's vital interests were at stake, Nehru forgot lofty sentiments . . . and subjected himself to the charge of inconsistency. His policy is either Machiavellian or statesmanlike, according to your point of view. Our conscience may gag at it but on the other

28   *Ibid.*
29   Reinhold Niebuhr, "Politics and Morals," *Messenger*, XXII (January 1, 1957), 5.

hand those eminently moral men, Prime Minister Gladstone of another day and Secretary Dulles of our day, could offer many parallels of policy for Nehru, though one may doubt whether either statesman could offer a coherent analysis of the mixture of motives which entered into the policy. This is beyond the competence of very moral men."[30]

Nevertheless, Niebuhr sees American foreign policy as gradually maturing in an era of world responsibility. He believes the Congress and our people are capable of vast generosity and good will. The citizens of the nation must have wider loyalties to values that transcend the national interest. In the Marshall Plan and in assistance to nations who sometimes vote against us in the United Nations there is a blending of self-interest and idealism, of love and self-love. "Ideally the presuppositions of Biblical faith insist on both the moral imperative of the love commandment and the fact of the persistence of self-love in actual history. There is, in this faith, therefore, a safeguard against both sentimentality and moral cynicism. This must be made available to the nation in the present period of critical decisions in which we cannot afford to disregard either the moral possibilities or the moral realities of our common life."[31] The gravest threat to the wise employment of those resources is moral self-righteousness. Pride and self-centeredness lie at the roots of both isolationism and imperialism. The former is the selfishness of the weak, the latter of the strong. "When we were tempted to isolationism, the Christian and secular idealism which sanctified this attitude was intent on proving our nation more moral than other nations because it did not become involved in their quarrels. Now that we are tempted to imperialistic domination of the weak nations by our strength,

30 Reinhold Niebuhr, "Kashmir and Nehru," *Christianity and Crisis*, XVII (March 4, 1957), 18.
31 Reinhold Niebuhr, "Our Moral and Spiritual Resources for International Cooperation," *Social Action*, XXII (February, 1956), 18–19.

another form of heedless idealism tries to sanctify our position. We equate a rigorous opposition to communism at all costs with 'morality' and accuse our allies of 'expediency.' "[32]

These views, sometimes expressed with polemical force, are in keeping with the Anglo-American tradition. Their lasting value is to remind us of both the possibilities and limitations of moral idealism in statecraft.

Winston Churchill shares with other spokesmen of the Anglo-American tradition a healthy regard for working principles in international relations. "Those who are possessed of a definite body of doctrine and of deeply rooted convictions upon it will be in a much better position to deal with the shifts and surprises of daily affairs than those who are merely taking short views and indulging their natural impulses as they are evoked by what they read from day to day."[33] To begin with, this doctrine entails an understanding and agreement on where the nation is going and some form of consensus on the national interest. Again and again, Churchill rose in the House of Commons to say: "It is evident that the parties in the House agree on the main essentials of foreign policy and . . . moral outlook on world affairs."[34] For Churchill, it was also possible to say, "The vast majority of the people of this country are united on fundamentals."[35]

Those who quarrel with this view delight in pointing out that different national leaders and political parties give the national interest different interpretations. Churchill acknowledged differences in detail but asserted, "The deep purposes of great nations are not . . . governed by the ebb and flow of political discus-

32   Reinhold Niebuhr, "Coexistence or Total War?" *Christian Century*, LXXI (August 18, 1954), 971–73.
33   Winston S. Churchill, *The Second World War: The Gathering Storm* (6 vols.; Boston: Houghton Mifflin Co., 1948), I, 210–11.
34   *Parliamentary Affairs*, Hansard, Vol. 413, August 16, 1945, p. 95.
35   *Ibid.*, Vol. 446, January 23, 1948, p. 556.

sions. . . ."[36] Britain as every nation was obliged by geography
and interest to range its objectives in hierarchical order. Its
paramount foreign policy was the maintenance of an equilibrium
of power in Europe. In the words of Churchill's colleague and
faithful deputy through the war years, Lord Avon (Anthony
Eden): "The foreign policy of this country has been based on
the determination that no one country should dominate Europe.
. . . It is for that reason that there were wars with Philip II of
Spain, with Louis XIV, with Wilhelm II, and . . . with Hitler
and the Third Reich."[37] For more than four hundred years,
England has opposed any power which threatened domination
of the Continent. The strongest, most aggressive nation, regard-
less of ideology, has been the object of resistance. The old guide
was the security of Europe, and no account was taken of *which*
nation it was that sought the overlordship of Europe. "The
question is not whether it is Spain, or the French monarchy, or
the French Empire, or the German Empire, or the Hitler regime.
It has nothing to do with rules or nations, it is concerned solely
with whoever is the strongest or potentially dominating tyrant."[38]
For Britain, this was a law of public policy and not an empty
category which sentiment or petty preferences could change or
control. In any concrete case, the task of the executors of policy
was to discern what nation constituted a threat through com-
bining massive power with the desire to dominate. Its wonderful
unconscious tradition required Britain to stand guard over the
balance of power and especially to deny to a potential aggressor
the control of key points, such as the Low Countries, in the
security of Europe.

The pursuit of its central national interest lodges the responsibility for the direction of foreign policy in the supreme civilian

36   *Ibid.*, Vol. 304, July 11, 1935, p. 549.
37   *Ibid.*, Vol. 408, February 28, 1945, p. 1514.
38   Churchill, *The Second World War: The Gathering Storm*, I,
     208.

leader. In war and peace, his is the task of interpreting and applying first principles. There is always the risk that military leaders, especially in time of grave crisis or military conflict, may usurp this authority. They complain of interference and speak of the political viewpoint as being an unmitigated nuisance. Yet war, like peace, is too serious a business to be left to generals. Even the most humane and public-spirited among them have far too vague and qualified an idea of the role of civilian authority. By their posture, they test the mettle and iron will of responsible leaders who must always be prepared to challenge their parochial and hidebound ideas no less than any other body of experts.

In the postwar era, Churchill found security for Europe and the rest of the world in the superior power and determination of the United States. One assurance of the maintenance of peace was the partnership of the United States and Britain. "The drawing together in fraternal association of the British and American peoples, and of all the peoples of the English-speaking world may well be regarded as the best of the few good things that have happened to us and to the world in this century of tragedy and storm."[39] If everything else failed, the best chance for survival rested in this alliance. The alliance was raised to the status of the supreme British interest primarily because it alone afforded effective safeguards for peace and order.

The alliance, however, is the core and not the totality of viable international security. In an earlier period, Churchill had declared: "I am for the armed League of all Nations, or as many as you can get, against the potential aggressor, with England and France as the core of it. Let us neglect nothing in our power to establish the great international framework."[40] Following World War II, he broadened the core of the international system. "If we add the United States to Britain and France; if we

39   Winston S. Churchill, Speech to the "American Society in London," July 4, 1950.
40   Churchill, *The Second World War: The Gathering Storm*, I, 210–11.

change the name of the potential aggressor; if we substitute the United Nations Organisation for the League of Nations, the Atlantic Ocean for the English Channel, and the world for Europe, the argument is not necessarily without its application today."[41]

Finally, Churchill's philosophy of international relations throws light on the procedural aspects of British policy and the spirit that informs its practice. The technique of "wait and see" is integral to its mode of action. British foreign policy is activated by a slow-burning fuse. For its critics this is an evidence of inertia; for its sympathizers it is a mark of *sang-froid*. A policymaker obliged to unravel the strands of conflict in the web of the international situation must, as the saying goes, have ice water in his veins. The problems confronting him are more baffling and perplexing than those by which Solomon was tried. He must deal not with the isolated problem but with a continuous succession of interrelated troubles. One of his most difficult problems is that of identifying the real threat to security. In practice there are countless perils, irritations, and dangers. Sometimes one danger must be tolerated and overlooked in the hope that an unfriendly antagonist may be beguiled away from possible alliance with another still more dangerous troublemaker. In the interwar period, Churchill observed with regard to Hitler and Mussolini: "Two dictators, men of unusual force and commanding ability, are saluting and embracing each other in Rome. But anyone can see the natural antagonism of interest, and perhaps of aim, which divides their peoples."[42] If Chou En-lai and Andrei Kosygin are substituted for Hitler and Mussolini, Churchill's principle has relevance today. The iron rule in the conduct of foreign policy is to increase dissension among your foes at the same time you are healing the divisions which inevitably arise among friends. Foreign policy is the enterprise of

41 *Ibid.*
42 Winston S. Churchill, Speech on "The Choice for Europe," May 9, 1938.

driving a wedge between your enemies and preventing them in turn from splitting the "grand alliance" you have created. Thus, while Churchill was unalterably opposed both for reasons of interest and power to military adventures on the mainland of China, he warned British critics of General Douglas MacArthur: "A wave of irritation is passing across the United States and the isolationist forces there are glad to turn it upon Great Britain. The reproaches against General MacArthur . . . enable those who do not like us in the United States to suggest that His Majesty's government has had something to do with General MacArthur's dismissal."[43]

In the foreground of any nation's foreign policy there are always certain basic interests vital to its self-preservation. Sometimes they are obscured in the drive toward policies of world improvement or in the dreams of world conquest. At other times they are repudiated in particular conceptions of foreign policy but unless restored by practical men can bring disaster. Germany, by courting conflict on two fronts in violation of the enduring interest enunciated most clearly by Bismarck, who had earlier warned against conflict with both Russia and France, brought about its own downfall. Spain, in the fifteenth and sixteenth centuries, by over-extending itself assured its decline as a major power. Every nation through its political leaders must engage in a continuous process of self-examination seeking to determine its vital interests.

Churchill described Britain's vital interests and those of the free nations as comprising three great concentric circles. The first was the British Commonwealth "with all that comprises. Then there is also the English-speaking world, centering upon the United States, in which we, Canada, and the other Dominions play so important a part. And finally there is United Europe."[44] It is the business of statecraft to discover to what extent interests are compatible and if they conflict how they may be rendered

43   New York *Herald Tribune*, April 28, 1951, p. 4.
44   *The Times* (London), October 11, 1948, p. 4.

mutually consistent. Churchill was persuaded that wise policy required Britain to pursue its actions at the points of intersection. "The three majestic circles are co-existent, and if they are linked together there is no force or combination which could overthrow them, or even challenge them effectively."[45] These mighty and august circles of interest formed a common front against imperialism in any form.

This framework for viewing the world is intimately connected with Churchill's profound grasp of the relationship between diplomacy and power. Surely the devotion and steadfastness of this doughty champion of freedom needs no defense. He stands supreme as the father of the doctrine that security comes only with strength and that the appetites of an aggressor feed on its success. His speech in Fulton, Missouri, on March 5, 1946, was the first clear warning that an Iron Curtain had been thrown up from Stettin to Trieste. It is often forgotten, however, that he counseled in that very speech, "What is needed is a settlement, and the longer that is delayed, the more difficult it will be and the greater our dangers will become." Again on April 18, 1947, at Albert Hall in a speech to the Primrose League he declared, "I say with all sincerity that our policy towards Russia must be one of honourable friendship from strength." The following year he said, "The western nations will be far more likely to reach lasting settlement without bloodshed if they formulate their just demands while they have the atomic power and before the Russian Communists have got it too."[46] On December 10, 1948, he summarized his thinking by saying: "I have frequently advised that we should endeavour to reach a settlement with Russia on fundamentally outstanding questions before they have the atomic bomb as well as the Americans. I believe that in this resides the best hope of avoiding a third world war."[47] By the early 1950's he had called on no less than forty occasions for an

45   *Ibid.*
46   New York *Times*, October 10, 1948, p. 1.
47   *Parliamentary Affairs*, Vol. 459, p. 721.

approach to the Russians aimed at a peaceful settlement. His counsel went largely unheeded; the opportunity he described passed us by, and the open sores of tension and division persisted.

However, the point is not to praise or blame Churchill or to justify him in the eyes of friend or foe. It is, rather, to suggest that this practitioner of statecraft whose position in history is firmly established as the symbol of the Anglo-American tradition saw no inherent conflict or contradiction between strength and negotiations. For many Americans unschooled in the lasting truths of statecraft, it remains a favorite indoor pastime to equate negotiations with appeasement. Successive administrations have been reluctant to state political objectives partly from fear of domestic political reactions. We have gone to "the Summit" for discussions with the Russians only when senators like the late Walter George provided the political support for this action, however ill-timed it might have been, however inept and miscast our tactics.

Fortunately, another great American, the late President John F. Kennedy, was constrained to declare, "We must never negotiate from fear; we must never fear to negotiate." And the present secretary of state, Dean Rusk, bred in the same tradition, offered this trenchant analysis on May 5, 1951: "We almost made the grade after World War II and almost succeeded in organizing the world to keep the peace. One rogue government stood in the way. Our reaction to this situation will determine our lot for an entire generation. We can keep trying and, with intelligence, patience and maturity, can succeed in producing such moral and military strength in the free world as to make it unassailable. We can fail miserably if we let our glands determine our action, decide that any agreement equals appeasement, grit our teeth and say that any fight must end only in the unconditional surrender of one side or the other, and 'go it alone.' I see no quicker road to total savagery nor no surer way to destroy this country." President Lyndon B. Johnson's offer of "unconditional negotiations" derives from the same enduring tradition.

Americans confronted with the gravest crisis to civilization that mankind has known are not bereft of a living tradition to guide and inform the approach to foreign policy. We are not impoverished in thought nor lacking in doctrine. We are the inheritors of a proud legacy of prophecy and practice. At times its precepts are drowned out by popular and demagogic creeds. Sometimes it finds little favor with the ordinary citizen, hard pressed by immediate needs. Yet it awaits in each generation men of courage who will speak plainly to the people. The Anglo-American tradition is not a recipe for easy success. It offers no simple and self-enforcing answers. For every crisis as for every life there is a time to speak and a time to be silent, a time to negotiate and a time to remain firm, a time to act and a time to wait, a time to live and a time to die. Someone in full command of the changing situation must make the decision. The rest of us must have confidence in his integrity and good judgment. This is made easier to the degree we grasp reality, replace emotion and hate with reason and restraint, and move ahead. There are moral and political resources both explicit and implicit in the Anglo-American tradition. We do well to feed on the wisdom of its wisest spokesmen rather than being swept along by the latest headline.

III

THE CHANGING DIMENSIONS
OF POLITICS AND MORALITY

What set them [Americans] apart from the rest of the world was important yesterday. What seems important today, on the other hand, is what is common to us all.

LUIGI BARZINI

CONTEMPORARY society is ill at ease about the relationship between its prevailing customs and practices and its moral standards. The fact is that men in every age share a sense of guilt and uneasiness when they contrast what they do with what they believe they ought to do. Evidently, tension between the *is* and the *ought* is inescapable. Societies discover, however, that the gulf separating norms and behavior must be kept within limits if life is not to become intolerable. Historically, man has most often tried to cope with this tension and contradiction in one of two ways. Either patterns of conduct are transformed to fit moral standards or standards are trimmed and adjusted to accord with behavior. The modern world offers countless examples to illustrate each form of adjustment. One or the other may be fostered or made possible by changing circumstances or new insights and perspectives.

Respect for individual worth and human dignity rests at the heart of the Judaeo-Christian tradition. It is inherent in the guiding philosophy of Graeco-Roman thought. It is basic to liberalism, humanism, and democracy. Yet, for more than two thousand years slavery persisted; the rights of women were disregarded; child labor was countenanced; prisoners were abused; the poor, it was said, would "always be with us"; the ignorance of the masses was considered inevitable; and health and well-being were reserved for the few. Today no enlightened leader or responsible citizen can any longer settle for the past. Poverty, ignorance, and disease are targets of national policy. Equality of opportunity has crowded out servitude and slavery as the working principle by which respect for human dignity is being legislated. Women have come into their own. The statute books are crowded with administrative rules and regulations controlling child labor. From Jeremy Bentham to the American Law Institute's most recent penal code, prison reform has become a staple of legislatures and courts. Poverty is no longer foreordained. Free and compulsory public education is everywhere enshrined. Health and well-being are recognized as central to "the good society."

The changes which have taken place gradually and almost imperceptibly are now so commonplace that few persons, if any debate the issue of improving individual welfare. When reactionaries from time to time challenge the applicability of social policies to serve the individual in one or the other sphere, they seldom enjoy a respectful hearing. The force of growing moral consciousness coupled with the pressures and programs that give it content and form have compelled the largest segment of mankind to bring practice in line with principle. Circumstances and the context of contemporary life have inspired a transformation through which societies in these areas at least have successfully narrowed the gap between the is and the ought.

This is, of course, only part of the story. There are other realms in which the tension has if anything become more acute. Practice in highly competitive sectors of the economy, with their stringent criteria of profit and loss, has complicated the pursuit of righteousness and integrity. Cutthroat competition remains a part of today's lexicon. Big government makes development of civic virtue and public responsibility more difficult. The emancipation of family life from a simpler and more traditional pattern and the freeing of men and women from ancient constraints have encouraged a reexamination of sex and morality. Respect for the individual, including the self, is not made any easier by the anonymity of urban life. And in a thermonuclear age, critics ask what has happened to the sense of moral revulsion to war, to a renunciation of the acts and means of violence, or to the compelling lesson that man should love, not seek to destroy, his brother? The buildup of armaments, the growing intensity of ideological and political warfare, the sharp differences between the meanings nations give to the same words and concepts—all point to the chasm that divides the world. Democracy, freedom, socialism, imperialism, and justice take on the appearance of large earthen vessels into which nations pour the contents of separate streams of thought and practice. The United Nations has found that human rights mean different things in the Communist and non-Communist worlds, and even broad and general resolutions have raised problems for the world assembly.

There are fundamental differences then between the two responses that have been delineated. One points to success in legislating morality; the other finds a way to live with injustice. In one, the growth of moral consciousness and the compulsion of changing circumstances help in the building of new laws and institutions. In the other, efforts to outlaw warfare or legislate social custom and behavior remain a dead letter on the books. What are the elements of difference? How can we account for the divergence? Why do practices move upward toward principle in the earlier sphere and principles devolve to accord with practice in the latter sphere? What are the factors which explain these differences?

The focus of this study is politics and foreign policy, which are the stage on which statecraft continues to be practiced. Exploring this realm may illuminate the problem. The adjustment of practice to morality versus the adjustment of morality to practice is broader than international politics. Other approaches in other areas could equally well be made. In the end, each approach must draw its justification from knowledge and convenience. To look at the changing dimensions of ethics and politics, including world politics, the observer must be prepared to ask the hard questions. These include questions on the nature of man, the essence of politics, and the conduct of foreign policy.

MAN

The starting point in a discussion of ethics is always man. For two thousand years the debate over forms of government and order has taken as its base line, expressly or by implication, the search for an answer to that baffling question, What is the nature of man? What is the proper end of man? Some have found the answer in the words of the Westminster Catechism: "It is to love God and serve Him forever." Others conclude that life by its nature is poor, nasty, brutish, and short. Some see man as hopelessly driven by forces beyond his control: history, the means of production, vitalistic impulses, power, ambition, anxiety, supremacy, acceptance, survival, security, status, gain, avarice, mores, myths, organization, or ritual. Others prefer to believe that man is master of his fate through reason, will, commitment, faith, consent, judgment, dedication, authority, or virtue. The debate on the ends and means of government is rooted in the nature of man. The political consequences of competing doctrines of the nature of man determine what societies conclude about the polity.

So we appropriately begin by asking what we are to think of man. Yet the beginning is but the first step in a long journey. Every answer involves us in paradox and contradiction. Who would quarrel with Reinhold Niebuhr when he writes: "If man insists that he is a child of nature and that he ought not to pretend to be more than the animal, which he obviously is, he tacitly admits that he is, at any rate, a curious kind of animal who has both the inclination and the capacity to make such pretensions. If on the other hand he insists upon his unique and distinctive place in nature and points to his rational faculties as proof of his special eminence, there is usually an anxious note in his avowals of uniqueness which betrays his unconscious sense of kinship with the brutes."[1] Or who in holding up the mirror would deny that, "If he believes himself to be essentially good and attributes the admitted evils of human history to specific social and historical causes he involves himself in begging the question; for all these specific historical causes of evil are revealed, upon close analysis, to be no more than particular consequences and historical configurations of evil tendencies in man himself. . . . If, on the other hand, man comes to pessimistic conclusions about himself, his capacity for such judgments would seem to negate the content of the judgments. How can man be 'essentially' evil if he knows himself to be so?"[2]

Man indeed is his own most vexing problem, for he is both good and evil, rational and compulsive, generous and grasping, compassionate and cruel, human and divine. It is the special character of politics and international politics to write these qualities large, not to create or produce them. Nor can philosophers or statesmen ignore the truth that never in history have good and evil been distributed between two lumps of mankind or two groups that deserve to be called children of light and children of darkness.

1   Reinhold Niebuhr, *The Nature and Destiny of Man* (2 vols.; New York: Charles Scribner's Sons, 1945), I, 1.
2   *Ibid.,* 1–2.

On the contrary, each individual is capable of infinite kindness and unspeakable brutality. And the great societies who historically comprise mankind must bear the same burdens and strengths. Thirty years ago, the most cultured nation in Europe sent six million Jews to their death. Twenty years ago, the most humane of civilized nations was first to use the atomic bomb. A story is told of the early death of a particularly winsome youth. The mother and her friends, desperately seeking an answer, finally declared, "God took him from us because he was too good." For long minutes his old and wise father listened patiently and then replied, "Yes he was a good boy . . . but not that good."

The defect in every religious and political view which sees man as wholly good is its partial and limited view of man. Each of us is at war with himself and with members of his society. And, we must add, at war with the society in which man's best acts are lesser evils. As Paul confessed, so must we all confess that "the good that I would I do not: but the evil which I would not, that I do" (Rom. 7:19). Whatever our better motives and intent—and who can read them fully—factors conspire against us and forces drive us along. We are propelled by preoccupation and haste, pride and self-interest, obsessions and uncertainty, ignorance of the facts and their consequences, and a flow of events which escapes our control. Our virtue and our wisdom are tested not once but repeatedly, relentlessly along the continuum of every so-called simple life choice.

The trouble with every simple-minded formulation of a program of moral goals translated into political terms is the self-destructive character of the goals. Those who believe that the Good Life or a viable political order can result from concentration on a single goal are condemned to disillusionment and failure. We fight for virtue not on one front but on many. It is tempting but hazardous to ignore this in ordinary family relations where the parallel with politics is limited but nonetheless instructive. The most poignant testimony in the Warren Commission Report is that of Lee Harvey Oswald's mother. In words which should be emblazoned on the memory of every earnest parent, Mrs. Oswald declared that she had used her strength through every waking hour to earn a living for her family. There was no time left over for the expression of sympathetic counsel or understanding love. Her worthy but insufficient goal drove her to neglect a youngster who with every month and year felt more rejected. The moral is clear that seeds of rejection were planted not from evil intent but from a mother's single-minded purpose which was too exclusive, too all-consuming, and too incomplete.

On the level of policy and statecraft, a similar moral may be drawn both from Nazism and communism. For Nazism, the goal of a superior human organism justified the extermination of millions of Jews as "a necessary hygenic measure." Marxism, too, seems to be an attack on one facet of the human problem as a remedy for all else. A bourgeois economic order leads to class struggle and social injustice. Rectify this and the state as well as man's exploitation of man will wither away and disappear. No price is too great for this single purpose. Social and economic justice pursued single-mindedly without regard for other individual rights led to the destruction of six million kulaks in Russia —peasants who stood in the path of economic progress. It engendered a moral fervor which in the name of a single goal swept aside all other moral purposes. The dialogue between Churchill and Stalin at a wartime conference is perhaps history's most dramatic statement of ruthlessness engendered by a too narrow moral and political cause. When Churchill pursued the issue of how many lives could justifiably be sacrificed to the reconstruction of Communist society, Stalin half-seriously acknowledged that there was no limit. In relations among states, the moral crusade can be destructive whenever a state in pursuit of a single goal wipes out other worthy ends. Freedom must be preserved by those who strive for equality; peace must be recognized by those seeking justice; and order must be established if democracy is to have a fair chance. The United States strives to bring an end to colonialism but is also a member of NATO; it seeks to reduce the threat of nuclear warfare but erects a shield against expansionism through its atomic arsenal; and while resisting communism it supports change in certain Communist states. For the United States as a world leader justice and power can never be wholly separable. Power does not create justice, but justice without power is impotent. Often the highest good for states must be the law of distributive justice. Fences may not make good neighbors, but their absence can often intensify enmity and tension if rights and responsibilities are left vague and unclear.

Men of good will and noble aspiration are required not only to cherish and extend their vision of a new and better world but also to live with those whose visions may not be identical with theirs. They must master the art of putting themselves in another's place—see the world through the eyes of De Gaulle, Kosygin, even Chou En-lai. This is the lesson in world politics which the condition of men and nations makes abundantly clear.

The irony of political and social decisions is the illusive quality of virtue and its resistance to every abstract and single-minded expression of good intent. The good life for a man's family may be sacrificed to earning a good living. The prosperous and proud, self-contained family and nation too readily ignore the rest of mankind. We live our days in our several communities: the family, our business, the locality, our nation, and the world. Even assuming we were as virtuous as we claim to be, each community confronts us with its powerful and overarching demands. Who has not known the responsible and respected leader whose family life was an empty shell? Or the loving father whom colleagues knew only as a heedless and ruthlessly self-seeking entrepreneur? Or the nation which in seeking its "good ends" wreaked havoc across the face of the globe?

Yet, even if man is not wholly good or if national virtue is lacking, man's spark of the divine is never snuffed out. An earlier newspaper account of the planned assassination of the then Attorney General Robert Kennedy is filled with deep meaning and pathos. The reportedly hired assassin—a hardened and experienced criminal—confessed that one experience deterred him. He was unable to carry out his sordid task because, as he prepared the crime, he caught sight of the Attorney General's family at play. For him this experience touched a chord more deeply imbedded in his character than he knew.

The Scriptures, of course, pay tribute to the notion of man— miserably selfish and parochial—transcending himself by God's grace. The secular world pays homage to this truth when it speaks of someone in the grip of a great idea. Men have thoughts; ideas have men. Even here, we ignore at great hazard and final disillusionment the fact that great deeds find their impetus in frail and base human motives. Winston S. Churchill caught this truth when he declared, "Ambition and pride are goads to every lasting accomplishment." The blending of lofty and seamy purposes is the clue to moral conduct. Our great theologians, such as Paul Tillich, know this better than those who give us daily doses of personal and political moralizing. History records the fact that morality is as likely to die at the hands of self-appointed moralists as of cynics and critics.

The perils of self-righteousness and religious pride are always with us. Pietists and literalists are seldom the architects of the good society. Each religious and philosophical tradition must acknowledge that none has a monopoly of moral insight. Protestants should acknowledge that Jews in this century have often possessed a more fervent sense of justice. The Catholic tradition has spoken with greater force on the restraints of warfare and has said emphatically that force must be proportionate to the objectives sought or defended. Tillich has written of "those who worship God without ever speaking his name." "For as many as are led by the Spirit of God, they are the sons of God." (Rom. 8:14) And in philosophy and theology we have a rich heritage of writings on practical morality drawn from the Greeks. Let us turn more directly to a discussion of ethics and politics and draw some conclusions applicable to foreign policy.

POLITICS

Each observer translates his concept of man into the realm of politics. The Founding Fathers translated their thinking into the living reality of the American constitutional system. Was it not Thomas Jefferson who observed that if man were wholly evil, no government would be possible. If he were completely good, no government would be necessary. Since man is both good and evil, the structure of government must channel his virtues and reduce and contain his vices. The answer for the master builders of American constitutionalism was a government reflecting an equilibrium of powers and checks and balances. It was a system in which the ends of man were enshrined in a higher law and a Bill of Rights. Representative government from that time to the present, on the national and international stage, has undertaken to do justice to these truths.

Or in practical terms, politics must do justice to both the competitive and cooperative instincts of man. All too often, education and philosophy today seem to equate progress and virtue with freedom from rivalry. Power politics retains its sinister and evil ring. This is an era of happy adjustment and of amity through repose. Even religion has been seized by the prospect of bargain basement peace of mind and the comforting promises of positive thinking. We seek to rule out competition, deny its necessity or existence, or dampen it down. If men are inherently reasonable, why must their claims be stretched taut by tests of influence and the struggle for authority? Yet, any parent knows the reality of sibling rivalry, the striving for personal identity, and the eventual reaching out by every normal child for his place in the sun. Every student of politics knows the contest for recognition, influence, and justice between labor and management, white and black, rich and poor, north and south, east and west, or state and nation. In politics every option is conceivable, and each program awaits its prospective champion.

Beyond this, in a democratic era, the domestic or internal

politics of foreign policy is a permanent reality. Every government looking outward has its domestic front. Perhaps in an
earlier and simpler era of aristocratic elite, this fact was less
self-evident. In the mid-twentieth century, the politics of leaders
is deeply ingrained in foreign policy decisions. Examples are
as numerous as international problems. American Presidents like
Franklin Roosevelt and John F. Kennedy apparently discussed
quite frankly with foreign leaders the problems they faced in
international negotiations because of the domestic political scene.
As a young Congressman, the Philippine leader Macapagal had
promised constituents that the Philippines would never give up
its claim to Sarawak and Sabah. At the Little Summit Conference
in the summer of 1963, his pledge was a source of division with
the new Malaysian state. Most national life is forever in the grip
of the politics of alternatives. The appeal of frustrated and dis-
illusioned intellectuals in South Korea for a new order or an
admittedly tenuous reunification is a policy alternative with which
Korean leaders and western diplomats are obliged to live as are
student political demands for continued hostility against Japan.
More positively, our hope in the cold war for the Communist
states is grounded in the struggle for contending forces leading
to a more healthful evolution and toward new alternatives. What
western leaders fear is not competition within the Communist
world but its more dangerous and uncontrollable forms. Competition within closed societies leading to greater responsibility is
the hope of the future. This may be truer today in Eastern Europe
than elsewhere in the Communist world, but who can say where
change will be most pronounced in the future? Our sole concern
is that events not get out of control and lead threatened and
anxious governments to acts of desperation and escalation of
the conflict from which the free and the enslaved world would
suffer equally.

Even for open societies in their relations with tyrannical states,
competition plays a useful role. If there had been no competition

with the Communist world, Europe might not have known the Marshall Plan and its unprecedented economic reconstruction. Rivalry provides incentives for men and states to be more virtuous and more united than they might otherwise be. The social revolution we are witnessing for equal opportunity in our own land is a case in point. So is the test we face from the Marxist creed and prophecy. Marx believed that the rich would become richer and the poor poorer until capitalism fell of its own weight. A moderately progressive social movement in the 1930's was America's answer to this challenge as were the social and economic programs in other industrialized countries. Today the challenge is the Leninist version that rich nations will become ever richer and poor nations poorer, coupled with Trotsky's assertion that the road to Paris and London is through Peking and Calcutta. This second great challenge is more serious, far-reaching, and ominous. No nation is rich enough nor any people generous enough to solve the problems of others. Yet, short of this, the rich nations have much to offer in experience, tradition, technical assistance, and human capital. Before we withdraw from the struggle, we would do well to recall that we are the carriers of a permanent revolution. Our own great transformation has occurred in the twentieth century. In 1900, one out of five infants died at birth while today one of forty perish. In 1900, one or two of one hundred houses had electric lights. Americans in the last sixty years have concluded that poverty was not foreordained, that all men would rather be fed than hungry, educated than ignorant, properly housed than in slums, healthy than ill, rulers than ruled, and participants than pawns. The experience of our own unfinished society, always in "process of becoming," is meaningful therefore to rich and poor alike, to new states as well as ancient ones.

But if the life of politics is competition rather than repose and if progress emerges from strife, cooperation, on the other hand, is also part of the fabric of American society. Man is a social animal. Voluntary organizations are a continuing part of the landscape visible to De Tocqueville, who spoke of Americans as joiners, and to Reisman and MacIver. But a more fundamental aspect of cooperation in American politics is the existence of standards. There has always been tension between pragmatic political acts and our higher philosophical and spiritual principles. Contemporary constitutional principles have been measured against the higher law. We test each legal issue against living American doctrines, such as the presumption of innocence, the right to vote, and the protection of the individual through a host of constitutional safeguards. For every new voting system, legislative device, and economic arrangement, Americans assume some underlying rationale or justification. The Founding Fathers linked the American Constitution to the higher law and to certain objective standards of truth.

This tradition makes international cooperation in its broadest sense congenial to the American experience. The same necessities that spawned our system are paralleled in the United Nations. The preamble and Articles 1 and 2 of the Charter are consistent with American political theory. Our corporate goals are found in the American Declaration of Independence and the Bill of Rights. The Charter is the first draft of the corporate goals of an emerging international society. It was and is illuminated by flashes of documentary lightning over the ages—English and Colonial, Greek and Roman, legal and theological. Mankind needs time— our most precious commodity—to build similar structures and traditions for the world. Some measure of progress in furthering the peaceful succession of leaders and governments, the balancing of order and justice, and the quest for rule by consent of the governed around the world are essential to the growth of a stable and just international order. In the vast unstable and volcanic areas of underdevelopment which are populated by 70 per cent of the world's people, there is need for new and more imaginative machinery of technical assistance. Some of our leaders are right in sensing that great upheavals and profound shifts of political affiliation are possible here as the pressure of poverty and the rejection of helplessness whip them into action. A silent and far-reaching revolution has engulfed the world and men are no longer resigned to remaining backward, poverty-stricken, or un-lettered. In these areas, national technical assistance is often not enough; international cooperation is called for and required. The most urgent needs of reconstruction and assistance to the devastated and starving masses are more than a great power responsibility. Following World War I a single nation, the United States, through the missions of the late President Herbert Hoover, was able to serve a broad segment of the suffering peoples of Europe. It is a sign of the times that with growing international solidarity, international obligations have been transformed. The common welfare is the primary concern of the United Nations, the International Bank for Reconstruction and Development, and other international agencies. Without abandoning its goals and values, the United States through successive postwar administrations has seen fit to work through broadly based international organizations. This course calls for wisdom and restraint, great skill and sophistication, and recognition that the facilitating agencies will come from the international community. Yet in countries that retain suspicions and sensitivity to national programs of outside assistance, this fact can be a blessing. Part of the process of American maturity has been the growing awareness that we appear at our best in the role of partner, rather than patron. This is partly because the recipients of our help are caught in the predicament best described in the statement, "Do a man a good turn and he will never forgive you." Irritating as it may seem to the generous donor, governments in poorer countries will suffer embarrassment and possible defeat if they acknowledge too openly their dependence on others. Their plight is exploited by a political opposition. Thus in dealing with foreign aid, both those who give and those who receive grow ever more impatient, the one because he is unable to justify to himself and others the many forms of unrequited love and the other because he cannot afford to acknowledge his debt.

FOREIGN POLICY

Let us turn from politics to the broader realm of international relations in foreign policy. The ethical dimension, as men measure and interpret it, commonly takes on one of two colorations. We are told either that nations must be moral, presumably as a particular man's nation is moral, or, on the contrary, that morality for states is a practical impossibility. Both outlooks are unequivocal. In neither can the problem be seen in any shade but black or white; and given the original premise, one can state each case in logically consistent terms. At one extreme, is it not indisputable that the values which guide national leaders are part and parcel of their national heritage? Do not these leaders acknowledge that the ends they seek are a product of national tradition and national interest? Is not truth for a nation in practice most likely to be found in the slogan "my country right or wrong"? When it comes to popular regimes and the wellspring of their morality, who is to challenge the affirmation of the leader of Italian fascism—"sixty million Italians can't be wrong"? Indeed, can it not be said that utopians who would refashion the world in their own image have much in common with self-seeking leaders who defend aggression as an expression of national destiny? The essential similarity between the two is a belief that justice is possible among states only if the national ends and goals of a particular leader and his state prevail. Fantastic as it seems, Woodrow Wilson—if only in this respect—shared a common outlook with Hitler and Mussolini. He saw the concepts of the New Freedom, especially as they were evolving in the American system, as the only means of transforming an evil and selfish international system into a just world order. International morality for him, if it were ever to be realized, would require a strong injection of American morality.

At the opposite extreme, critics of Wilson then and now point out the futility of every naïve attempt to establish an international morality. The search for morality among nations is largely a mischievous and pointless venture. Moralism is a façade behind which nations pursue selfish ends. Ethics are in practice ideological rationalizations by cunning leaders who seek to justify what they do. Nationalism becomes in practice not so much love of country but love of more country. Not only does the leader who has frequent recourse to moralisms mislead friend and foe, he also confuses his own people. Necessary practical measures are transformed into holy doctrines that grow rigid and frozen as guides to conduct. People are lulled into believing that a single noble and enlightened course of action solves the problem of discovering a rational foreign policy. Like the adversaries in the American Civil War, they see what they are doing as absolutely righteous and beyond the test of prudence and political judgment. In all this, they deceive themselves and reduce the freedom of action so necessary for strategic and tactical moves on the chessboard of international politics.

Experience indicates that somewhere between moralism and cynicism, an ethical dimension exists now as in the past. A long history of enduring political writings makes this clear. So does the insatiable quest of man for justice. It is true that decisions in foreign policy seldom involve simple or tidy choices. With all our predilection to praise or blame policy-makers for the practice or abandonment of righteousness, we know that foreign policy is a complicated business. Actions stem from on balance judgments. The actors must sift a myriad of facts and a vast collection of conclusions from the facts. It is difficult to talk about ethics in general whether in terms of peace or justice or international order. A more appropriate posture is one which sets out to examine each specific and concrete case. What is needed is a cool evaluation of the elements involved in a decision and the consequences likely to flow from each alternative course of action. Sometimes the best may be the enemy of the good. Not absolute truth but practical morality must be the guide. In Jacques Maritain's words, "Means must be proportioned and appropriate to the end, since they are ways to end, and, so to speak, the end itself is in its very process of 'coming into existence.' " And such a view of foreign policy must give heed to the call for restraint, a sense of proportion and prudence. With John Dewey, we can say that "means and ends are two names for the same reality." Proximate morality may be the highest attainment in statecraft.

The focal point of moral purpose in international relations is the interests and goals of a nation. We start with the tacit assumption that responsible men will, broadly speaking, view national interest in similar terms. If this were not so, bipartisanship would be impossible. The present secretary of state has observed that he has appeared before committees of Congress in executive session from one hundred to two hundred times. He is able to recall only two occasions when the discussion of important issues was cast in partisan terms. On both sides of the aisle the controlling viewpoint was "what is right for the country." Congressmen off the hustings seek the best interests of their country. The Englishman T. H. Healy wrote to Lord Hugh Cecil, "Nationalism is what men will die for. Even the noble lord would not die for the meridian of Greenwich." If the national interest doesn't exhaust the possibility of ethical principles, it is always the necessary starting point.

This fact should never obscure the need for a decent respect for the opinions of mankind. If it is possible for political leaders to think responsibly about the national interest, they can also be expected to search for common interests with the spokesmen of other national states. If national interest is a fact, so is the mutuality of national interests. There are common interests transcending narrow national interests. They form a network of shared relationships that draw together men of different national creeds and aspirations. For example, Germany today is sharply divided into opposing political systems. No one expects the differences between East and West Germany to dissolve overnight. If change can be expected it will come from a series of "little steps" or technical changes that may draw the country together or encourage a political settlement. Trade, cultural exchange, and limited tourism may, if practiced with patience and restraint, unlock the doors to greater unity. Even when existing political systems divide, common social, cultural, and economic interests may in time serve to unite.

No division is more profound and no cleavage greater than that separating present rivals in the arms race. Looking out over the chasm that divides East and West the late Secretary General of the United Nations Dag Hammarskjöld put forward a design for disarmament by "mutual example." He queried whether the Soviet Union and the United States did not have a common interest in limiting their armaments and checking their spread to other powers. History will show that the great powers have inched ahead in the limitation of armaments. Bilateral disarmament in certain fields preceded the nuclear test ban treaty. There have been tacit agreements to limit at certain points the further accretion of certain forms of military preparedness. There has been in recent years a corresponding respect by both sides for territorial boundaries in Western and Eastern Europe. While negotiators have failed or have not tried to arrive at an overall peace settlement following World War II, the crises in Hungary and Cuba demonstrate a rough-and-ready acceptance of the hegemony of the other side in its own sphere of influence.

Finally, international society is not bereft of certain broader principles of justice, freedom, and order. Their form may be embryonic in a half organized world, but their existence is understood. States in formulating their foreign policies seek points of correspondence between what they do and the broader principle. In foreign policy the concept of elemental right and wrong is never fully realized, but it can be approximated. Even the fact that states possess an awareness of injustice indicates the possibility of justice in foreign affairs, for a sense of injustice presupposes categories of justice to which leaders have recourse. Anti-colonialism is firmly rooted in certain general and inchoate notions of what is right. Often the right is but dimly perceived. Frequently, distributive justice is the highest attainment of states. The right may be as hazy and unclear as the shadows on Plato's cave. Yet these shadows are the beginnings of the necessary conditions for greater justice in the relations between states. As Reinhold Niebuhr has observed, "Our position is not an enviable one. Yet from an ultimate standpoint it need not be regretted. For a nation which cannot save itself without at the same time saving a whole world has the possibility of achieving a concurrence between its own interests and the general welfare; which must be regarded as the highest form of virtue in man's collective life." Order is the framework for the healthy growth of viable nation-states. A respect for national independence demands an international order to safeguard it. Freedom and justice presuppose order. If the world and its staunch supporters cannot preserve the international order, an early casualty is bound to be the survival of new and independent states.

Thus, there are layers of ethics in politics and international affairs. They deserve study especially when the strongest voices are crusaders and cynics. The ethical dimension is comprised of shades that are not black and white. Grays predominate; and, practically speaking, the characteristics of political ethics may be discoverable in the recognition of the relatives of all ethical judgments. The centers of morality and religion in the land cannot stand aside from man's needs in this realm. For example, the church which teaches patience in all things should strive to inculcate this attitude toward world affairs. Foreign policy all too often is like a woman's work—it never ends. As every long-suffering homemaker knows, even freezers and dishwashers have not changed this fact. And in much the same way, the shining United Nations' buildings, multilingual translation apparatuses, and instantaneous communications systems around the world have not prevented one challenge or conflict from following close on another. The consequences of actions that were noble in themselves are seldom fully anticipated. For example, a well-deserved homeland for suffering and persecuted Jews has led to new tensions in the Middle East. The French Revolution brought in its wake Napoleon's armies on the move across Europe. Independence for the newer nations in our day is only the beginning of new trials and testing. "It is provided in the very essence of things," Walt Whitman declared, "that from any fruition of success, no matter what, shall come forth something to make a greater struggle necessary." Most of life is lived on the ground of successive crises. Peace and prosperity in an "America sailing on a summer sea" never provided the acid test of character. Rather moral and spiritual resources are put to the test when loved ones depart, when peoples or nations teeter on the abyss of disaster, or when decisions have to be made for which there is no present consensus nor future certainty. Ethical judgments, however painful and difficult, often reach a high point in clarity and resolve at the moment of moral crisis.

POLITICS AND MORALITY IN A WORLD OF CHANGE

The rapid shifts and changes in the context of present-day international relations lead spokesmen for and critics of morality to opposing conclusions respecting the continuing relevance of morality and religion. Some spokesmen whom with a certain irreverence I have called idealists and apologists envisage the solution in a straightforward revival of religious consciousness. In a world dominated by a vast pluralism of religious and political outlooks, this approach seems more a pious hope than a practical possibility. But the answer of critics and cynics who rejoice in the passing of the Judaeo-Christian era is more disturbing. Who can take heart that a recent Gallup poll found that 62 per cent of 1,177 college and university students polled across the nation believe religion is losing its influence. Religion and its lessons provide a thread of continuity in a world of unsurpassed change. These lessons give us a theme on which discussion appropriately reaches some concluding points of focus.

Morality has served throughout history as a guiding force in relations among men and nations in three significant ways. It has deepened understanding of the nature and destiny of man. It has given standards for individual conduct including that of individual statesmen. It has maintained a continuing tension between temporal programs and the standards by which they can be measured.

Inevitably, modern man is tempted to question the continuing relevance of these three historic functions of morality and religion. He tends to see mankind as being or becoming either wholly good or hopelessly evil. If he holds the former belief, he is likely to choose a political system based on absolute majority rule; if the latter, tyranny or despotism. By contrast, the Founding Fathers, whose philosophy was informed by Judaeo-Christian and Graeco-Roman thought, held that man was both good and evil. If man had been wholly evil, no representative system would be possible. Since he was both good and evil, political institutions were devised to harness his virtues and limit his vices through checks and balances and the separation of powers. American constitutionalism rests on a more or less explicit concept of the nature of man. It assumes that man is neither totally depraved nor infinitely perfectible. In this it offers a viewpoint that has not lost its continuing validity.

Likewise, the historic function of morality in guiding individual conduct continues in our day. The far-reaching changes in warfare, technology, and politics have complicated the problem of individual responsibility. Who bears the almost unbearable burden of deciding the great issues of war and peace? Is it the President, the secretary of state, or the ambassador? Or are we all slaves to military authorities who determine the limits of national security? Or has the ebb and flow of public opinion become sovereign? To what extent are all of us carried along by forces we neither created nor can control? Who speaks for Americans and for mankind as a whole?

At first glance, men and nations seem tossed like floating wreckage on the waves of circumstance. If we take a second look, however, decisions are made by solitary leaders who act as best they can. They and we can only hope that the story will in the end come out right. They are judged in their daily affairs by some of the standards we use to measure neighbors and friends. An ancient adage says, "A diplomat is a man sent abroad to lie in the interests of his country." Harold Nicolson has amended this to read, "but he must also return to negotiate another day." In practice, the leader is judged by those with whom he deals and by standards not alien to the rules of decency and propriety recognized throughout society. Can he be trusted? Will he keep his word? Does he have a conscience and a sense of justice? At the level of working diplomatic relations, the homely tests of mind and character by which all men are judged do come into play.

Finally, the building of new societies is sometimes seen as diverging from the concept of two worlds or from the classic doctrine of the two swords under which men owe allegiance both to God and to Caesar. Throughout Africa and Asia, the most urgent need is to build a unified nation and to mold from diversity one people. This goal, while essential, is insufficient. If justice and equality are to prevail, proximate moral and political acts must have standards by which they can be judged. A voting system or a new legislative device is a practical political measure. It must rest on judgment and political wisdom. But the underlying principles on which policies are based, if they are to serve present and future generations well, must be measured against some higher law. Today, as in the past, there must be a continuing tension between the pragmatic actions of the political kingdom and the principles of a higher spiritual and philosophical realm. It is the higher principle of justice defined as "giving each man his due" which is forever in tension with constitutional practices and policies. The presumption of innocence, the right to vote, and constitutional safeguards of individual rights are more than political stratagems. They are working principles that have their origin in transcendent notions of justice and equality.

These doctrines and this creed that relate morality to life as a transcendent but relevant dimension of existence are neither obsolete nor dead. Their necessity is greater by virtue of the strains and pressures of a revolutionary age. The one thread of continuity in a changing world may be the relation of an objective moral order to the political order including the international order.

It would be tragic if in the discussion of new approaches to moral problems these insights were forgotten. On every front, there is today healthy ferment and vital debate on moral theories. Issues which preoccupy our foremost moral philosophers emerge in lively discussions on the new morality and contextualism and in the writings on existentialism. Current thought has thrown into question past approaches and assumptions. We have learned that abstract moralism divorced from concrete human problems offers little guidance. Our best observers of social behavior are continually pushing forward the frontiers of knowledge that illuminate the wellsprings of conduct. Through their efforts, not motivation alone but also the varieties of social relationships are seen more clearly. Their findings are grist for the mills of ethical theorists; it will no longer suffice to call for virtue in social relations without heeding the context and complexities of moral decisions. If anyone doubts this, let him examine the literature of sex ethics, business ethics, or political ethics.

Notwithstanding, alongside the directions inherent in this trend, moral maxims, precepts, and law itself, seen in the context of social reality, are being reasserted. If the dynamics of man's relationships in the social, economic, and political order require study and review, the penetration of these realms by moral perspectives, including objective moral standards, demand attention. It is clear that the stuff of human conduct with all its ambiguities and conflicts takes on meaning from the observer's angle of vision. Behavior is not a given. Its reality from the standpoint of ethics depends on moral perspectives. To understand ethical conflicts, the observer must ask ethical questions, and these require insights that never wholly derive from the situation. Facts do not exhaust our approach to reality. It does not follow that because we have discovered more about human situations with all their complexities that those who strive for clarity on ethics can abdicate ethical positions. Ethicists in search of relevant principles discover them in the situation only to the extent that they are continually involved in testing the relevance and relationship of moral perspectives to conduct. It remains true in an age of exploding knowledge about mankind that the social situation is no *tabula rasa.* Nature, including human nature, speaks to man only if man asks appropriate questions of nature; and these questions depend on the observer's perspective.

The realms of national and international ethics are no exception. Two examples may serve to illustrate the problem. In civil rights, the achievement of social justice depends finally on human conscience working itself out in a complex cultural and economic order. It is difficult to legislate respect for others especially when one group of citizens fears the encroachments of another group into areas long controlled by deep-seated dominant social mores. Yet we know that civil rights legislation and underlying objective standards are providing incentives for mutual respect that is otherwise lacking. Changes in voting rights, better housing, and equal opportunities for education and employment are spurred by law and principles of justice. Objective principles of justice are embodied in social legislation that show the first signs of influencing behavior.

On the international scene, objective standards may play a similar if more limited role. The least publicized but most far-reaching program of the United Nations may be the work of its economic and social agencies. The circumstances of desperate need for two thirds of the world's people stimulate these efforts, but so do the purposes written into the Charter calling for social and economic advancement around the world. There can be no disputing the fact that today human needs are better understood, but the response of the international community results as much from the declared goals of newly created international institutions as from anything else. The founding fathers and institution builders had redress to timeless principles of justice and respect for human dignity that provided the working principles for an advancing international society. It is in this sense that objective principles are relevant to the changing dimensions of human need. In these terms, the international order is related to a higher moral order.

IV

A VIEW FROM
THE TWENTY-FIRST CENTURY

*We are set on a conspicuous stage and the whole world marks
our demeanour.*   EDMUND BURKE

WE live in an era of unbelievable and perhaps unbearable
change. Institutions and practices that have withstood the test of
centuries are being challenged on every hand. No adjective has
become more commonplace in the twentieth century than "obsolete." Among the institutions said to be out of date are the
free market economy, the sovereign nation state, the family, and
the self-reliant individual. And when we protest that time has
not destroyed the timelessness of, say, sovereignty or individual-
ism, we know this is only partially true. Time does "make ancient
good uncouth."

Prediction and reading the future while standing on the quicksand of an age of change are particularly difficult. Landmarks are few. We take readings from bench marks that are passing from view. The rate of development is more likely to be geometric than arithmetic. Unanswered is the question of whether rapid physicial or social change has reached a plateau or is destined to accelerate. A more puzzling question is, will change in one cultural sector induce change in others. Prophets are not at their best either in highly static societies on the threshold of long postponed development or in those turbulent eras which offer little of permanence on which to stand.

Yet, whether history is predominantly changing or static, it possesses both elements of continuity and change. No period has been wholly lacking in one or the other. Even the most dramatic forms of change do not dissolve the bonds that link men with their past. States and individuals soon learn to live with their past. The past and present are joined inextricably in the future of mankind. In any present, patriots live and die knowing their deeds will live after them. Old men plant trees they will never see full grown. Young men fight wars for national traditions shaped by their forefathers and not themselves. History is a seamless web in which past and future are knit together through the labors of the present.

Moreover, history is of a piece because those who mold it participate in mankind. They belong to the human race. Some men may be better educated, more progressive, better housed and fed, and healthier if not happier. Others are born to a lifetime of misery, poverty, and disease. Others may stand on the threshold of unrivaled well-being throughout the world. They may join in spreading a spirit of greater respect for the well-being of mankind or share a sense of resignation that civilization is doomed to decline and destruction. But man, with all his hope and despair, triumphs and failures, joys and disappointments, vision and short-sightedness, is man. The great recurrent theme in history is man himself. The forms and modalities change, but man is the fixed quantity with which analysis and prediction must come to terms. No reminder is more necessary for a time of flux and breathtaking change.

Change and continuity are the threads by which the fabric of every historical epoch is woven. In succeeding eras, the pattern is many-colored and varied. Sometimes the strains of flux and permanence seem blurred and indistinct, resisting those who would draw them apart. At other times the forces of change are overwhelmingly dominant. Occasionally, past, present, and future are so interlaced that continuity alone prevails. Nevertheless, history moves along through a blending of the old and the new, the fixed and changing. Anyone who would understand a period like our own must hearken to both. The postwar years are unquestionably revolutionary, accompanied by sweeping transformations around the world. A survey of the cold war must begin with change, for it has engulfed all mankind north and south, east and west. Yet, when we are done with change, we must leave time for continuity, for in a quite basic way it too is a part of the warp and woof of the present era. Ancient forms and practices persist. The new is also a reflection of the old. Modern representative government in the West shows traces of a feudal order. Traditional societies live on in the present-day autocracies of certain new states.

REVOLUTION AND CHANGE

If there was ever an era in which the historian had to face the challenge of measuring great massive social forces, it is the one in which we live. This is an era of multiple revolutions which have shattered, but not destroyed, ancient and traditional societies. The great transformations which are shaping the future and with which we must come to terms are the technological and military revolutions, the political revolution, and modernization as a worldwide process. Each is a product of far-reaching forces; each has momentous consequences for the future.

The first of the great transformations is that wrought by technology. Communications have too often brought people together not as friends and close neighbors but as porcupines huddling together in a moment of terrifying fear and mutual awareness that their fate is interdependent. Transportation has annihilated distance. A flight from Tokyo to New York or from New York to New Delhi takes fourteen hours by commercial jet or just about the time required to travel a few hundred miles fifty years ago. It takes less time to cross the Atlantic by sea than was required to cover the distance between Philadelphia and Washington a century ago.

Technology also affects the news we read and the literature that shapes our thinking. The American press follows us wherever we go. Books and libraries in every country in the world bear the trademarks of American publishers. From Bangkok to London, we find well-stocked collections of American writings.

Every minute of the day, the American republic is represented at ten to twelve international conferences by instructed American delegates. Men are coping continuously on a worldwide basis with problems which span national boundaries and spill over from politics and diplomacy into technical, economic, social, and scientific areas. Commissions and fact-finding agencies are at work around the globe. Diplomats labor around the clock as commanders of fire brigades. Secretary Rusk was at his desk fifteen months without a day's respite.

No one can avoid looking back to an earlier and simpler era without a certain sense of nostalgia. Thomas Jefferson's correspondence as secretary of state reveals a troubled man complaining that for more than two years nothing had been heard from the American consul in Madrid. He goes on to say that if no letter were forthcoming the following year, he intended to do something about it. Today the Department of State receives 1,300 incoming cables and sends out approximately a thousand on every working day of the year. It is charged with the protection of American interests, whether of tourists traveling abroad or businessmen taking part in $20 billion of exports or $15 billion of imports. It carries on political relations with more than one hundred nations—a third of which change governments each year. Today, the British Ambassador to the United Nations files his cables to the Foreign Office in London at the end of each day. His messages await colleagues in the Foreign Office when they appear at work the following morning. They go about their task throughout the day, answering his requests for instructions and information; and by the time he returns to his desk the following morning, their answers are on his desk. In the modern era, diplomats have been transformed into minute men working in their operations room around-the-clock; and this, of course, puts an immense strain on those who carry the very heavy burden of office. Their sense of urgency is linked with the high stakes of the game, for warfare, which has always been viewed as a pursuit of diplomacy by other means, has become overnight a contest in finding ways to prepare something that may lead to ultimate, mutual destruction. Consequently, the profoundest expression of the technological revolution is in the realm of military affairs.

If one looks back to the writings of earlier military historians, he observes that they were not at all in favor of battles, especially at the beginning of the war. In fact, one particular general wrote that "I am even persuaded that an able general can wage war all his life without ever joining battle." Mercenaries, who were the chief export of countries like Switzerland, passed from one employer to another; and men in arms served side by side with future enemies. This temperate and moderate approach to conflict was drastically altered by the French and American Revolutions. The *levée en masse* and the nation under arms replaced professional armies. A new era, as Marshal Foch wrote, was ushered in. Wars no longer were carried on for dynastic interests, for conquest of a province. Instead they were fought for the spread of philosophical ideas. This revolution and its effects on warfare were the results of the convergence of very far-reaching changes, each reinforcing the other. Modern warfare involves the engagement of a whole people in a struggle for a total philosophical and religious system, facing one another with absolute weapons. It is no longer restricted to a handful of mercenaries fighting without deep commitment for successive kings.

This combination of forces has utterly changed and modified the picture of conflict. We underestimate the scale of this revolution if we merely speak of weapons five thousand times as destructive as the one used at Hiroshima. We shall have ignored the full emotional and human character of the problem, a problem which will not yield rapidly to exhortation or injunction. Not only are weapons more destructive but so are the national emotions that give them impetus. Yet, ironically, this very destructiveness can in the hands of rational men inspire new restraint and responsibility.

A second great revolution has occurred, supporting and reinforcing the first. It is the political revolution both within and among nations. Its ingredients within nations involve once again the replacement of professionals in foreign relations by the people, by hundreds of legislators and thousands of newspaper readers, all of whom see themselves as makers of foreign policy. Foreign policy is no longer the business of an aristocratic elite who speak the same language, read the same books, trace a common lineage, and share common goals and aspirations. This new form of foreign relations moves the conduct and evaluation of policy rapidly toward a football stadium psychology where the public keeps score, chalks up victories and defeats, and chooses heroes and goats. In such an atmosphere, strategic advance and retreat are equated with virtue or vice; caution is seen as cowardice; and patience, firmness, and respect for the interests and opinions of others require elaborate justification.

What leaders say or are provoked or induced to say oftentimes goes far beyond any reasonable prospect of success. In consequence, we face the problem of forcing our spokesmen to speak with two voices: one for their professional colleagues, and another for those who demand from them strong words, strident emotions, and even belligerency and bombast in the face of an enemy.

The political revolution has also changed the anatomy of decision in foreign policy. Leaders operate in a nexus of inter-related decisions and consultations. Policy-makers must touch base at numerous points in the system. The present process has made the secretary of state or even the President more a sheep-dog than a leader. He becomes the man who tries to rally support behind a policy which is continuously being reformulated along a changing front, causing our friends abroad to ask at any moment in time, "Where is the point of decision in a foreign policy question?" "Who speaks for the nation?" "Who represents American policy?" "Where is the center of gravity in any given crisis?" Diverse and varied agencies in government each have their foreign commitments and their own independent centers of gravity. Viewing this growing network, former Secretary of State Dean Acheson once observed that no secretary had been in full control since 1900.

This whole internal revolution has meant that the business of the Department of State, which thirty years ago required a budget of $14 million now exceeds $300 million for normal operations, and in the broader foreign relations field is infinitely greater if we consider the more than $100 billion provided in foreign aid since World War II. The military budget is con-tinually mounting, and numerous private and public efforts multiply around the world. Out of five million civil servants, three and one-half million are involved in military preparedness; and one million Americans represent us abroad in one capacity or another. The amount of machinery the government needs to carry on relations with the rest of mankind dwarfs all that had been known in an earlier day.

But the political revolution within nations is matched by a far-reaching revolution among nations. More than one billion people have received their independence from former colonial forces, and nine hundred million more have come under Communist tyranny during this period. The full extent of the political revolution can be measured only by the interaction of these far-reaching changes, these two movements in history.

Even under the most ideal conditions, the process of orderly and peaceful change would have been difficult, but it has been immeasurably complicated by the clash of communism and democracy. Ambassador Charles Bohlen, at the time he was our envoy in Moscow, declared in a speech to Foreign Service officers in Washington that "instead of devoting its influence to the promotion of orderly and harmonious changes, the Soviet Government appears to be pursuing exactly the opposite task in seeking at every point to influence existing grievances, to create hatred where none exists, and to perpetuate the resentments for past injustices into the future."

And if in 1965 one were to substitute China for the Soviet Union, and apply Ambassador Bohlen's description to Vietnam, Laos, and other trouble spots in Asia, he would have a fairly accurate description of the present conflict.

Thus, a new colonialism has arisen simultaneously with the de-colonization that has taken place through resolute efforts in another part of the world; and this, it seems to me, represents the second great transformation of our time.

The third world revolution is the process our social scientists have described as modernization. They note that an even more universal and worldwide transformation than democratization or communization is taking place. Universal patterns of modernity are affecting all mankind. Modernization spans diverse values, institutions, traditions, and religions. It has its origin in Greek science and the natural theology of Western Europe in the twelfth century. While it has made its greatest strides in unlocking the secrets of nature, it also manifests itself in the reform movements in religion and in the scientific, technological development in the realm of material advancements. A dialogue between Gandhi and Nehru is instructive here, for when Gandhi

wrote to his heir apparent, "If India is to attain true freedom
. . . people will have to live in villages, not in towns," Nehru
replied, "I do not think it is possible for India to be really
independent unless she is a technically advanced country."

Modernization has led everywhere first and foremost to inte-
gration and centralization of policy-making; and gradually the
private realms of transportation, communications, business, and
education have been brought under public control. Functions
once the province of the tribe, family, or locality have been assumed by the state. Even where governments have deliberately
pursued policies of decentralization in particular realms, as with
agriculture and education in India, with its centralized economic
policy, the pressures of modern life have led more and more
toward centralization in all fields. As life becomes more complex
in modernized societies, all human actions come into contact
with the law at some point or another. The legal system grows
and with it controls from the center.

In economics, modernization brings technological improve-
ments which lead to increased production through increased
mechanization of labor. Rapid growth in per capita productivity
follows. This, for the modernizing state, increases the gap between its economic status and that of the more traditional societies. It tends to widen the gulf between the rich and the poor.

Per capita income in advanced countries where modernization has gone furthest exceeds $2,500 while in traditional so-
cieties $50 to $100 is the annual income. Per capita income in
many countries of Latin America is less per year than it is per
month in this country. There are changes in other realms, in
social structures, where peasant societies long isolated are becoming urbanized; where two thirds of the people crowd together
in cities; where literacy, which had involved less than one half
of the people, becomes universal; where the divisions between
peasantry, townspeople, and an aristocracy disappear; where individual achievement rather than inherited status plays a determining role; but where the countervailing force of great amor-

phous, anonymous aggregates of people counteract the more healthful effects of modernized living. The strains are greater, moral confusion is increased by the breakdown of traditional values, the process is more abrupt and less uniform for the new as compared with older states, and the gap between aspiration and attainment cannot but breed discontent. At best, the student of modernization must settle for on balance judgments. It is progress but not utopia, opportunity but not continual betterment, and withal an enhancement of the capacity for both good and evil.

LIVING WITH PRESENT REVOLUTIONS

What does the observer have to say about these far-reaching transformations? What can education offer? What can the informed leader bring to bear? It seems to me that he must attempt, first and foremost, without reference to religious, philosophical, or political prejudice, to describe changes as they occur and to free minds as much as possible from the fettering controls of dogmas which distort the value of these transformations. No one can be neutral about the great values men and nations espouse, but he can be detached and objective in appraising their political and international expressions and interaction.

Secondly, in each realm the leader and his fellow citizens have the task of fashioning institutions and techniques that will mitigate or cope with these worldwide and all-pervasive transformations. Certainly, it ought to be the business of education in an interdependent world to speed communications of ideas across national boundaries and to extend the outreach of peoples in all nations, both in professional and technical areas, at the level of citizenry, and in all the arenas of life where understanding is essential. In addition, on a much sterner and harsher level, is it not the business of education and science to find ways of communicating intention and capacities in war and peace in order to minimize the possibility that great lethal weapons might be used to incinerate the entire inhabitable portion of the world—

devices such as the hot line between Moscow and Washington, D. C.?

All these very flimsy but nevertheless essential tools for communicating man's real intent toward his adversaries, as well as his allies, come into play. Certainly, the historian and political theorist has a duty to clarify the relations between ideals and religious convictions on the one side and political action on the other. He should remember, too, that when these relationships are tightly and narrowly hedged about by crusading, political outlooks, the whole process of understanding and accommodation among people—as in the case of the American Civil War—breaks down.

Third, in the realm of communications, is it not important, likewise, to probe new forms and methods of diplomatic accommodation and adjustment among people? The evolving machinery of parliamentary diplomacy is the most visible form of this new technique. Parliamentary diplomacy has come to be used in the broad sense to describe the practice of intergovernmental negotiations and discussions carried on under fixed rules of procedures in bodies like the League of Nations and the United Nations. Secretary of State Dean Rusk prior to his appointment to that high office provided the following working definition of the phrase:

What might be called parliamentary diplomacy is a type of multilateral negotiation which involves at least four factors: First, a continuing organization with interest and responsibilities which are broader than the specific items that happen to appear upon the agenda at any particular time—in other words, more than a traditional international conference called to cover specific agenda. Second, regular public debate exposed to the media of mass communication and in touch, therefore, with public opinions around the globe. Third, rules of procedure which govern the process of debate and which are themselves subject to tactical manipulation to advance or oppose a point of view. And lastly, formal conclusions, ordinarily expressed in resolution, which are reached by majority votes of some description, on a simple or two-thirds majority or based upon a financial contribution or economic stake—some with and some without a veto. Typically, we are talking about the United Nations and its related organizations, although not exclusively so, because the same type of organization is growing up in other parts of the international scene.[1]

The United Nations by now is a continuing organization with 117 members including—by contrast to its predecessor, the League of Nations—all but a handful of the most important nation-states. Its existence dictates that a majority of foreign offices conduct a significant fraction of their international business within the United Nations framework. The smallest of the new states may in fact at particular moments have as many officials at work in United Nations organs and agencies as serve their governments in foreign ministries at home. Beyond this, countries like the United States annually participate in 350 to 400 international conferences with delegates instructed by their government on a long list of agenda items. In the setting of international conferences, the representative must practice the arts of both the negotiator and parliamentarian.

Ambassador Charles Dawes is quoted as saying, "Diplomacy is hell on the feet," to which a colleague replied, "It all depends on whether one uses one's feet—or one's head." Parliamentary diplomacy puts a still greater premium on using one's head. For Demosthenes the first duty in politics was to be "in control of occasions." There is a time to act and a time to wait, but the question is always which is it? There is a time to debate and a time to negotiate, a time for firmness and a time for conciliation. If states are willing, the world forum can be used to promote international cooperation, but it can also be used for national propaganda. "When the foreign minister of a great country mounts the . . . world platform and when he states a position in the name of his country, . . . when he attacks . . . the position

1 Dean Rusk, "Parliamentary Diplomacy—Debate vs. Negotiation," *World Affairs Interpreter*, XXVI (Summer, 1955), 121–22.

of other countries, and when the dispute touches upon the very basis of the political regimes to which he finds himself opposed . . . , it is rather difficult . . . the next day to say 'I was mistaken.' "[2] Often when a delegation is unwilling to negotiate in confidence, they employ an international assembly as a sounding board. In 1954, the Soviet Union showed its hand at the Berlin Foreign Ministers' Conference on the prospects for an Austrian Treaty and German reunification by launching a propaganda broadside against the West. Large international congresses are as subject as the U.N. to such abuses. Reviewing the early years of the United Nations, Paul-Henri Spaak declared: "I have often wondered . . . whether we have not pushed open diplomacy a little too far and have not sometimes made it more difficult to arrive at a solution by making public everything that we said and did within the diplomatic framework."[3]

The rise of the newly independent states has magnified the prospect that the United Nations will be used as a sounding board. Nations that are emerging from the breakup of the British, French, Belgian, Dutch, Portuguese, and Spanish empires have found a readymade instrument for speeding the liquidation of empire. The once secure majority of the United States and its European and Latin American friends in the General Assembly has ended. It is tempting, with the tide running against the United States, to suggest a curtailment of the use of the worldwide forum. Sober thought leads to the opposite conclusion, however, if the goal is to bridge the gulf between old societies and new or between the Atlantic community and the developing world. To ignore or seek to stifle a tumultuous parliament on the theory that he who is not my ally must be my enemy would be to resign world leadership in the vast reaches of Africa and Asia to the Soviet Union if not to Communist China.

2   Paul-Henri Spaak, "The Role of the General Assembly," *International Conciliation* (November, 1948), 613.

3   *Ibid.*

Nevertheless, if the situation does not call for an abandonment of parliamentary diplomacy, the friends of the United Nations have a duty to face the problem of how a multitude of governments can be saved from becoming a sometimes irresponsible mob. In this task, "the dogmas of the quiet past are inadequate to the stormy present." Sydney Bailey has well said that the trouble with parliamentary diplomacy is that it has become "more and more parliamentary, and less and less diplomatic."[4] Debate has come to be viewed as an end in itself. It is forgotten that "the chief purpose of parliamentary diplomacy . . . is to cause a reassessment of national interests in the light of the national interests of others."[5] There are situations where mere discussion may prove useful, as in the General Assembly's handling of the Syrian-Turkish conflict in 1957 and the Security Council's treatment of the Sudan-Egyptian border dispute in 1958. Talk can serve as a poultice drawing the infection from a conflict. Yet the facts of a situation may call for more than this. There may be times when the findings of an international body must be supported by the power and prestige of a United Nations presence. Diplomacy historically has been validated by national power. Parliamentary diplomacy acquires force from the more subtle and intangible power of the international community. "A government may refuse to comply with a decision of a policy-making organ but would think twice before taking action which would bring it into direct, on-the-spot conflict with representatives of the international community."[6] To challenge a United Nations presence can be seen as an affront not to the power of a national state but to the full authority of the international society.

It is also true that parliamentary diplomacy suffers from a certain unwieldiness. It may not always respond swiftly to a crisis. Writing of national assemblies, Walter Lippmann observed, "The

---

4   Sydney Bailey, *The Secretariat of the United Nations* (Rev. ed.; New York: Frederick A. Praeger, Publishers, 1964), 42.

5   *Ibid.*

6   *Ibid.*, 43.

reason why we trust one man, rather than many, is because one man can negotiate and many men can't."[7] He added, "One diplomat may see what is in the other diplomat's mind, and time his utterance accordingly; a whole people cannot see quickly into another people's mind and its utterance is inevitably crude. The very qualities which are needed for negotiation—quickness of mind, direct contact, adaptiveness, invention, the right proportion of give and take—are the very qualities which masses of people do not possess."[8] Nations, including those in Asia and Africa, are not oblivious to this fact. In 1957 as tension mounted between Thailand and Cambodia, they turned not to the General Assembly or the Security Council but to the secretary-general. Then, and again in 1962, they asked for a personal representative of the secretary-general who might work with them in resolving their dispute. In taking action in 1957, with the knowledge but not the approval of the Security Council, Dag Hammarskjöld explained in his Annual Report that "such actions . . . fall within the competence of his Office and are . . . in other respects also in strict accordance with the Charter, when they serve its purpose." This philosophy undergirded Hammarskjöld's visit to Laos in 1959, his successor's appointment of a temporary executive for West Irian in 1962, the dispatch of United Nations observers to Yemen in 1963, and the mission appointed "to ascertain the wishes" of Sabah and Sarawak in 1963.

Another situation which impairs successful negotiation is the illusion that the United Nations is strengthened by throwing on its table a maximum of international business. Overloading the agenda may have the opposite effect. Negotiation takes time, and agreement is often a dividend of patience. The impression grows apace that the General Assembly in particular now tries to do more than it can do well. It has infrequently found ways of dispensing with "the old reliable" problems, like Southwest

7   Walter Lippmann, *The Stakes of Diplomacy* (New York: Macmillan Company, 1915), 26.
8   *Ibid.*, 29.

Africa, universal disarmament, and colonialism. Serious students urge greater discrimination to avoid what some would call "irrelevance or tedious repetition." There are limitations on public debate, and once the parties have made initial statements in public session, efforts to narrow differences should go on in private. The secretary-general has appointed a committee to consider whether the General Assembly might not delegate some of its powers, especially in peace-keeping, to a small representative group. The League of Nations went further than the United Nations in the use of special *rapporteurs* capable of elucidating the issues and examining possible solutions. Individuals are frequently able to succeed where committees fail, whether as the secretary-general or as the chosen instruments of an organ of the United Nations.

Parliamentary diplomacy can also help to keep open the channels between rival powers in world politics. Leaders of the great powers may in speeches, press conferences, or interviews signal that they are prepared to negotiate. Then, within or outside the United Nations, alert diplomats move to explore the prospects of agreement. The classic case is, of course, the settlement of the Berlin blockade in 1948–49 when Ambassador Philip C. Jessup successfully explored with his Russian colleague at the U.N. the meaning of a conciliatory statement by Stalin. Thus far diplomacy in the conference rooms and anterooms of the United Nations has filled in the gaps in contacts between adversaries in the cold war. Is it too far-fetched to ask, with American diplomats being expelled from countries in Africa and Asia, whether the United Nations may in the future provide opportunities for unobtrusive diplomatic contacts for countries separated not by conflicts between east and west but between north and south?

United Nations spokesmen have given appropriate emphasis to the strengthening of machinery for collective security and to developing and marshaling support for the United Nations Emergency Force. If, by its power, the United Nations has not

deterred many wars, it has helped to shorten at least four of
them: one in Indonesia in 1949, another between Arabs and
Jews in 1949, a third at Suez in 1956, and a fourth in the Congo
from 1960–64. The mid-twentieth century has witnessed less
the establishment of peace than a "general truce" in the cold
war and in specific conflicts such as the Arab-Israel dispute and
the war in Korea. Emerich de Vattel, in describing such a state
of affairs, wrote in one of his classic treatises on international
law:

> It [a general truce] scarcely differs from a treaty of peace, except
> that it leaves undecided the dispute which gave rise to the war. When
> the nations are weary of fighting, and yet can not arrive at a settle-
> ment upon the question at issue, they have recourse to an agreement
> of this character. It is thus that between the Christians and the Turks,
> instead of treaties of peace, truces for long periods are generally
> made. This is due sometimes to a false spirit of religion and at other
> times to the fact that neither side is willing to recognize the other
> as lawful master of their respective possessions.

Instruments of peaceful change and accommodation must be
adapted to the circumstances of a "general truce." They must
function in a world divided by "a false spirit of religion" and
recurrent disputes over the status quo. The United Nations is
probably incapable of establishing peace, but it has won its spurs
in the limitation of conflict. And lest this achievement be under-
valued or its price counted too high, we do well to recall with
Churchill that "a war postponed may be a war averted. Circumstances change, combinations change, new groupings arise, old
interests are superseded by new. Many quarrels that might have
led to war have been adjusted." In such a world, a parliamentary
forum must be the meeting place where any nation can talk with
its neighbors, where talks are never finally broken off, and where
issues, however insoluble, are never pressed beyond the point
where civilization is threatened. It must remain the scene of quiet
talks between the world's leaders no less than of lengthy prepared statements whether of hatred and mistrust or mutuality
and good will. "Though the U.N. cannot alter the international

distribution of power, nor even guarantee the weak against the determined depredations of the strong, it can mobilize and maximize the forces which in any given situation favor just or peaceful action, and can put at their disposal for this purpose the most extensive armoury of diplomatic and parliamentary devices so far known."[9] In this sense, parliamentary diplomacy carries hope for the future.

Beyond that, with reference to the far-reaching political revolution, ought not the task of all of us be to study the complex and awesome connection between democracy and foreign policy? If men of intelligence and learning fail to clarify in democracy the difficult process of making foreign policy in a public arena, then the risks of conflict multiply and grow. Was it not De Tocqueville and the authors of the Federalist Papers who said that democracy has none of the qualities essential to the efficient conduct of foreign relations whether these qualities be continuity, privacy, or moderation? Should it not then be the duty of all of us who must take a position and frame our beliefs in foreign relations, always to remember that we have not read the last cable; that progress in foreign relations, as in the welding together of a more enduring family union, is a slow, often painful and protracted business; that if we ask our leaders to accomplish what we in our day-by-day relations strive to do in quiet privacy without pitiless publicity and they fail, then the reason may be our asking of them what we know is impossible in other walks of life?

Moreover, ought we not in seeking to understand the political revolution as it has affected relations among nations, measure more clearly the problems of order and stability in the developing nations? These very fragile and emergent structures, whether we idealize or criticize them, have a life and character of their own that must be understood. Developments and changes in countries outside our jurisdiction yield slowly and imperceptibly

9   Herbert Nicholas, *The United Nations as a Political Institution* (London: Oxford University Press, 1959), 179.

to outside prompting and aid. The governments and societies of other lands are like plants. We are not their maker. Like a gardener we can patiently nurture them, tend them, improve the soil, and pray for the grace of kindlier elements. Above all, we can within the limits of our power serve and protect them, help rid their environment from weeds and disease that would choke their growth, guard them against unfriendly neighbors, and assist them in striking ever deeper roots in new soil.

Lord Franks recently observed that six battalions of the King's Rifles were the sole force of order and stability at one point in the mutiny of troops in East Africa. A thousand men in each battalion were rallied across vast expanses of country to maintain some kind of minimum order in a country that was no longer theirs, in which they were an alien force to the aspirations of many of the people, but where for a fleeting moment in history, there was still need for their functions in maintaining stability. Nations in larger and smaller regional groupings must discover or indeed recover forms of order and security appropriate to their needs.

We could go on in the economic realm to touch on the weaknesses of emerging nations, weaknesses which exceed mere statistical analyses. In terms of the best available indices, we are reminded that in the past five years, the increase in per capita income in the developed countries has been about $38; in undeveloped countries it has been $3, wiped out too often by rapid increases in population. Half the population of Latin America cannot read or write; only one in 800 has finished college; and infant mortality remains four times as high as ours. If we examine the gap between the rich and poor, the full extent of the problem between the developed and the undeveloped country becomes evident. It is a fact that economic growth, even in a country like Puerto Rico, rather generously supported by the largess of an immensely wealthy American economy, was outstripped five times by the per capita increase in the economy of the state of Mississippi, not ordinarily considered a particularly wealthy state in the American Republic. If this is the situation in Puerto Rico, a showplace of development, what must it be in less favored nations among less favored peoples?

So across a broad front, the world in which the educated and uneducated must live is a world in which, in a certain sense, the rich are bound to grow richer and the poor are bound to become poorer. If the informed do no more than paint the realities of this picture and sketch out the demands for aid and help in a rather desperate situation, their words of realism will have served a high and worthy cause. Yet a position of detached objectivity will not be sufficient. At a moment when many of us are tempted to stand aside from necessary sacrifices, we may forget that American aid represents about one half of one per cent of our gross national product, whereas France contributes more than 4 per cent of its gross national product. There is grave danger that in measuring our own efforts we may underestimate the sacrifices our friends and allies are making.

Finally, education can help men in our kind of world learn to live with the realities of continuity and change. If an illustration of the vagaries of change is needed, the present era would underscore it dramatically, for the jet plane and oxcart exist side by side in many parts of the world and rapid development is going on in many countries concurrent with slow, gradual and sometimes snail-like transformation. And if a further lesson is needed, it lies in the management of the cold war. The cry for change properly focuses on the need for new institutions and stronger, more unified, more modern forms of peace-keeping machinery, and ultimately some firmer structure of government. Yet while this cry goes up, we must remind one another that delegates and representatives of individual sovereign states in thousands of old-fashioned diplomatic meetings hammered out an Austrian peace treaty or a Korean armistice or a nuclear test ban. New as well as old forms of pacification and accommodation are needed.

Secretary of State Rusk has well said that there is utility in tedium and, further, that the business of marking out a viable relationship among nations requires continuity where the best man can hope for is that rivalry which cannot be erased can be mitigated, contained, or checked. Ancient as well as new institutions and practices must be mobilized for the management of conflict.

If these two precepts could somehow be filtered through the teachings of historians, political scientists, and the technicians in American education and learning, then perhaps not only the understanding of these three great revolutions, but also their control might be achieved through the better ordering and preservation of our common life.

CROSSING THE THRESHOLD OF THE TWENTY-FIRST CENTURY

As I write these words, which some might describe as essentially those of the pragmatic realist, I can hear a solemn warning from those who take the long view. The fact is that science is catapulting man across the threshold of the twenty-first century. All the changes portrayed above may pale by comparison with the future. Today a mere handful of nations has within their grasp the power to destroy one another. By the year 2000, many more may have this terrible ability. Since the close of World War II, two great powers have faced one another as the leaders and spokesmen for two grand designs to organize the world. Like powerful magnetic forces, they have for the better part of two decades drawn satellites and lesser forces into their orbits. Now the growing strength of other forces is reducing the gravitational pull. New world forces are emerging as new political planets and show signs of exerting their own magnetic attraction in the world. China is fast becoming a rival planet in the Communist world order, and an independent European center of power is foreshadowed in De Gaullist claims for a European place in the sun. A bipolar world is evolving in the direction of a multipolar system. In Asia and Africa, national destiny is linked less with the ultimate triumph of democracy or communism than the flowering of barely visible indigenous forms.

More fundamental perhaps is the challenge to a four hundred-year-old international system. Security from the time of the Treaty of Westphalia in 1648 has been safeguarded by the will and determination of sovereign states to protect their independence and territorial integrity. Interest in international politics is identified with national interest. History tells us, however, that larger regional unions and interests are possible if not inevitable. The idea of a united Europe, largely dormant from the end of the Napoleonic Wars to World War II, has deep historical roots. Medieval Christianity kept alive the idea of "the corpus Christianum," and the Holy Roman Empire was a political expression of a wider European dream. The idea of Mitteleuropa transcended the nation state as did the practices of the Concert of Europe. In the long view of history it may even be more accurate to see nationalism and national sovereignty as a brief interlude overshadowing for a few centuries the more enduring idea of Europe. If Asia and Africa have expressed their unities less fully, past and present forces exist which draw member states together and promise to gain strength in the future. The same can be said for Latin America.

More shadowy and less predictable are the political forms the new international order will take. No one can prophesy with much certainty the boundaries and structures of a restored European system. Indeed in the present world certainty is an illusion and the words of the great historian of modern Europe, Jacob Burckhardt, merit quoting: "A future known in advance is an absurdity." Will the new Europe fashion from its welter of competing national sovereignties a political system coterminous with its geographical, historical, and cultural boundaries? Will it reach out to embrace its separated neighbors in Eastern Europe? Or will divisions persist, old rivalries devolve into new ones, and modern civil wars supplant traditional rivalries? Can the nuclear age induce cohesion and a community inspired by interdepen-

dence and fear? Has the test of survival passed from the maintenance of national unity to the attainment of European solidarity?
Or will unity follow the historic route of domination by a major
power or the victory, as Marx foresaw, of a single ideology coin-
ciding with the demise of earlier forms, such as capitalism and
imperialism?

In Asia and Africa, the rallying cries for the moment are race,
anti-colonialism, or anti-imperialism. What will be their impact
on the emerging international system? How are we to judge the
warnings of historians like Toynbee that the future division of
the world may be in terms of race? Will leadership pass to the
colored race in building a new international system? Is the future
of mankind to rest with a numerically superior population long
held in bondage but now throwing off the shackles and achieving
a majority within present world forums? Or will the common
interests of mankind in social and economic well-being prevail
and add stature to the fledgling union of men of all races?

Our view of the twenty-first century is circumscribed by the
same risks that have imperiled political prophecy through the
ages. At best the contemporary observer looks out on history
through the glass darkly. It is tempting to assert that windows to
the future are clearer and less clouded than in the past.

No one questions that in certain broad areas we know more
about the world in which we live than men knew a century or
two ago. Statistics and knowledge of the past are more complete.
We have higher birth rates, lower death rates, and greater emi-
gration rates. The elemental factors responsible for the growth
and prosperity of nations are better understood and controlled.
Yet, although knowledge is greater, the facts that must be as-
sessed have increased in number and complexity to a bewildering degree. In place of the isolated rivalries of the past, we are
facing struggles that involve directly or indirectly the whole
habitable globe. Our problems have become so vast, their solution so painful and doubtful, and the weight of contingencies so
overwhelming that even for the wisest statesman foreign policy

is at least three-fourths guesswork. Moreover, for all our statistics, historical and economic knowledge, and responsible governments, we have had little success in foreseeing future events, let alone coping with present ones.

Failures in political prophecy are, of course, nothing new. History records countless examples of decisive political developments that caught even the most experienced observers by complete surprise. In the eighteenth century neither Benjamin Franklin nor Frederick the Great appear to have anticipated the approaching French Revolution, yet both were constant observers of the course of French affairs. Nor did someone as active in revolutionary politics as Madame Roland make a single allusion before 1789, in her voluminous correspondence, to the impending downfall of the French monarchy. Napoleon was confident that "Europe will be either Cossack or Republican," and Pitt prophesied that the end of the Papacy was in sight.

In 1760 Rousseau predicted that in twenty years England would have lost her liberty and been ruined. The statesmen of Europe joined philosophers such as Rousseau in proclaiming England a decadent and second-class power, a sort of insular Poland, selfish, faction-torn, without nerve or consistency, and destined probably to fall under Russia's domination. This illusion was shared by Joseph II of Austria, Frederick II of Prussia, and Catherine II of Russia. These erroneous estimates provided the basis for momentous policies which affected the future of the world. In much the same way, the Kaiser and Hitler underestimated both Britain and America and chose courses that changed the history of the West and of the rest of the world as well.

Philosophers and educators have failed most conspicuously to grasp the future—on the one hand, when they failed to allow for the accidental and contingent influence of unique personalities and, on the other, when the full thrust or the unforeseen decline of social or political movements escaped them. In an earlier age, too much stress may have been placed on the hero in history;

today we may be led astray by neglect of the possible role of a Churchill or a De Gaulle. The strong personality is still capable of altering the course of a nation's history—and thereby the history of the world. His passing may have effects no less profound.

The task of grasping the future requires not only a sense of the uniquely personal forces at work in greater or lesser leaders. It demands also a profound understanding of the prevailing tides of history and dominant social forces that characterize an era. The present age is one of multiple revolutions, shattering but not destroying ancient and more traditional societies. As we have seen, great transformations which are shaping the future and with which prediction must come to terms are the technological and military revolution, the political revolution, and modernization as a worldwide process. Each is a product of far-reaching forces; each has momentous consequences for the future.

Education which would help men to live with change must fashion the tools and concepts, the ideas and institutions for grasping and ordering the three revolutions. If educators are to prepare young men and women for the future, they must provide the means for understanding a dynamic present. This calls for a search for things which can be projected with some certainty into the future. It requires a clearer delineation of the tasks of social science and humanities. In an age where the physical sciences are catapulting man into the twenty-first century, the humane disciplines must look ahead—always as far as the state of their science or their art allows. In this spirit, those now at work in these disciplines may help all mankind to perceive and perhaps better to order and manage the future.

With all the difficulties that confront those who look ahead, a few propositions can be advanced, not without hesitation. Some of the world's problems that had seemed more remote will be in the forefront in the year 2000. The twenty-first century will find the peoples of the world living on a crowded planet. Not until the 1840's did the world's population reach a billion people.

Today's population of 3.3 billion is expected to double by the year 2000. By the end of the twenty-first century it will have reached 13.5 billion if the present rate of growth is sustained. According to the United Nations, there are 192,000 births every day or more than 60 million births a year, a figure which exceeds the population of Great Britain. The heavy birth rate, especially in the developing countries, and a steady drop in the death rate in modernizing countries are likely to continue unless a significant breakthrough is accomplished in population control. By the twenty-first century, the findings of science will help to reduce but not reverse this trend. The oral contraceptive and the interuterine coil will receive wider application as will newer and even more acceptable techniques. Pilot projects in population control in countries such as South Korea, Pakistan, and Formosa will be extended to other more difficult national situations. The fruits of family planning programs in countries like India with its expenditure of $56 million in the 1960's will become more apparent. Those who had opposed birth control on religious or cultural grounds will have adjusted doctrine to pressing reality. Throughout the twenty-first century, the work will go on and the dire prophecies of the experts will not be fully realized. But many will ask whether the effort has been too long delayed, whether it is not too late.

Today nearly half the world's population goes to bed hungry, and many suffer from chronic malnutrition. By the twenty-first century, important areas of the world will have suffered local and regional famines, first in Asia but later in Africa and Latin America; a tripling of present food production will be needed to feed the world's population. While the technology for this increase is available now, the peoples of the world will, for cultural and economic reasons, have proved unwilling or unable to adopt and apply it as promptly and efficiently as required. Nevertheless, food production will more than double in the next century, and better distribution and dissemination will be achieved. The food crisis will continue to be severe in countries like India,

Indonesia, and China where suffering is particularly acute in the late twentieth century. The findings of research centers, such as the International Rice Research Institute in the Philippines, which has demonstrated the methods and crop varieties that make possible the tripling of rice production, will gradually be applied and adopted throughout Asia; but governments and peasant farmers will lag in the use of new knowledge. Fortunately, the pressures of hunger and the enmities of race consciousness will not have merged to bring on a world war of the colored-have-not against the white-have countries as many fear. At a crucial juncture, the international community will have undertaken a massive program of sharing surpluses and skills, thus averting disaster.

Similarly, progress will have been made in controlling the hazards of nuclear warfare. An uneasy entente will have emerged between the United States and the Soviet Union. Europe, while displaying increased independence following the withdrawal of American ground forces from the Continent, will have continued its policy of cooperation within a loosely organized North Atlantic community. China, increasingly preoccupied with extending hegemony in Southeast Asia, will have moderated its policy of worldwide ideological expansion and control. Partly, its need to cope with massive national problems and, partly, the rise of a new generation of less doctrinaire Communist leaders will shape its policies. More and more, China will have been drawn back into the society of nations, first in more technical spheres and then as a member of the new United Nations. Moreover, the historic Chinese foreign policy of a loosely organized sphere of influence with major emphasis on its western frontier will have led it to accept neutral as well as client states within the range of its authority. Its advance will be checked by a concert of powers inspired by their own national interests, working within the United Nations, and including the United States and the Soviet Union.

The test ban treaty between the Soviet Union and the United

States will have proved to be a first vital step in armaments control. France and China and a small group of recent nuclear powers, for instance, Egypt, Germany, Israel, and Pakistan, will have accepted a stronger treaty for the limitation of nuclear testing. New machinery for policing the agreement will have been established, but uncertainty will remain because of a fear that countries such as China might find ways to test underground without being detected. Extensive powers will have been assigned to a supranational security organization, chosen by the members of the Security Council and General Assembly but freed from the control of the veto in certain limited yet vital areas involving nuclear armaments. The Economic and Social Council will have been revitalized and, with donor countries enjoying the benefits of weighted voting, have acquired an expanding role in aiding the developing countries. This shift from national to international programs will have come none too soon, for a sense of disillusionment and frustration will have set in among those who carried the heaviest burden of technical assistance. The new countries in Africa and Asia will have encountered numerous setbacks and failures in meeting the goals of economic plans. They will have grown quarrelsome and been willing too often to blame neo-imperialist scapegoats for all their failures. Their reactions will have strengthened the hand of critics of international cooperation, but sober leadership will have prevailed. Countries of the industrial north will have come to accept an obligation to assist on a more organized basis the nations of the developing south. Both will have banded together within and outside the major international organizations. New machinery will have evolved comparable to the Organization of European Economic Cooperation, but with countries like the United States and Canada as full members. The Soviet Union, which first took the lead in welding together the nations of Eastern Europe, will, with its growing independence and increasing relations with Western Europe, have taken part in joint discussions with members of the new northern regional organization.

Given the scope and magnitude of their needs, the developing countries will have lost much of their earlier suspicion and antagonism toward a broad regional organization. They will have found negative dividends in the earlier game of playing one donor country off against the other and will have recognized the pressures that have built up within the developed countries to halt all foreign aid. Then, too, they will be pleased that the new consortium of the more wealthy states has seen fit, once common objectives were established within the regional forum, to channel help through the Economic and Social Council and the World Bank. Here the claims and priorities advanced by African and Asian states will be placed alongside the programs developed by the capital-rich states. While donor states may often find these wider international forums cumbersome and unwieldly, they will have learned from experience that to ignore them could negate the purpose of their aid.

A few of the developing countries—Mexico, Pakistan, Nigeria, Brazil, and Chile—will have made dramatic advances. Others will remain caught in the grip of a vicious circle in which capital formation is delayed by the lack of internal savings. A few will seek to break this circle through tyrannical regimes which enforce hardships on the people by holding down standards of living, thus extracting savings for development. The majority, noting the evolution of societies in Eastern Europe, will choose to preserve some semblance of an open society. They will look, therefore, to the outside world, hoping with its help to break the vicious circle. The extent of their problem will be dramatized by the fact that an estimated 9 per cent increase in capital investment is needed to produce a 3 per cent increase in national income, which is precisely the amount needed for a country with an annual population increase of 3 per cent to hold its own.

Fortunately, progress will have been made, giving hope to those whose problems have seemed most hopeless. The Alliance for Progress will have demonstrated that for the somewhat more advanced countries of Latin America industrial and agricultural progress is possible. The twenty Latin American countries will have responded to public and private investments from the outside by generating the funds and human capital which more than match them. For approximately $10 billion of United States aid and $10 billion of private investment from Europe and the United States, the Latin Americans will have succeeded in raising some $70 billion in the 1960's and 1970's. Spurred on by this success, they will have found the human energy and economic skills necessary to become a genuine partner in the international economy. Their advancement will give hope to the countries of Asia and Africa which face greater cultural and economic obstacles and have further to travel.

Other changes will have improved the circumstances of developing countries. New and more efficient energy resources will have been discovered, especially solar and nuclear energy. Having been tried and tested at great expense in the wealthier countries, they will be applied directly in the newer countries, thereby shortcutting long stages in industrial development. More efficient methods will have been found for extracting food resources from the seas. Ancient practices will have been rediscovered, such as intensively cultivated fish ponds making possible greater exploitation of fish and vegetable matter. Wider use of fertilizers and improved cultivation will have increased available food resources; and projects such as the development of TVA-type operations in the Lower Mekong Valley and other places will have greatly spurred development.

However seriously we take this somewhat frolicsome excursion into prophecy, the facts are clear that great nations have found ways of cooperating with the historical process. History attests to the pivotal importance of small steps along the way. Wars and economic rivalries have a way of drawing attention from the deep undercurrents that carry mankind along. Viewed from the twenty-first century, these include a burgeoning world population, growing pressure on food resources, and national development in the more backward areas of the world. The spread of science and human knowledge knows no national boundaries. Raymond B. Fosdick, former president of the Rockefeller Foundation, reminded us in World War II that "an American soldier wounded on a battlefield in the Far East owes his life to the Japanese scientist, Kitasato, who isolated the bacillus of tetanus. A Russian soldier saved by a blood transfusion is indebted to Landsteiner, an Austrian. A German soldier is sheltered from typhoid fever with the help of a Russian, Metchnikoff. A Dutch marine in the East Indies is protected from malaria because of the experiments of an Italian, Grassi; . . . a British aviator in North Africa escapes death from surgical infection because a Frenchman, Pasteur, and a German, Koch, elaborated a new technique. In peace as in war we are all of us beneficiaries of contributions to knowledge made by every nation in the world. Our children are guarded from diphtheria by what a Japanese and a German did; they are protected from smallpox by an Englishman's work; they are saved from rabies by a Frenchman; they are cured from pellagra through the researches of an Austrian. From birth to death they are surrounded by an invisible host . . ." (Rockefeller Foundation Annual Report, 1944, pp. 9–10). The infinite threads that bind men together stem from their common humanity. They are the part of the iceberg below the surface. We see only the conflicts and tensions. A powerful nation must give expression to these enduring values. It must recall Pericles' warning: "I fear our own mistakes far more than the strategy of our enemies." It must never yield to the practices Thucydides described in Athens where "violence became the attribute of manliness."

As we look to the twenty-first century, the lessons of the past are relevant. Nations constrained by the imperatives of national security and threatened by hostile foes can choose craven withdrawal or cynical imperialism. But fortified by deep-running moral and intellectual resources, they can meet each new challenge, each successive moral issue. Our traditions and the force and energy of our people give us a fighting chance to realize this goal.

V

EPILOGUE:
MORAL RESOURCES AND STATECRAFT

The weaknesses of the nation are due to our frantic and nostalgic yearning after the original simplicities, for the sake of fleeing or avoiding present complexities.

REINHOLD NIEBUHR

HISTORICALLY, organized religion has been the chief home and defender of morality in statecraft as in other social and cultural realms. Intellectuals and philosophers as individuals have made contributions that loom extraordinarily large, sometimes as Christians, Jews, or Moslems but often as secular thinkers. This is because moral philosophy, like philosophy in general, has always required, in the words of William James, "an unusually stubborn attempt to think clearly." Men are unlikely to engage in this enterprise in mass numbers or even as individual spokesmen for an organized community or bureaucratic structure. Courage is required to wander off the reservation particularly if the wayfarer has any hope of wandering back. Our greatest leaders in the West have possessed this quality, but the fact that we commemorate only a few—like Lincoln and Churchill—testifies to the severe demands that society places upon them. It is simpler to defend, sometimes rather narrowly, the status quo or justify existing policies than to place them in their wider context.

Leo Strauss, professor of political philosophy of the University of Chicago, has argued that the goal of philosophy is to discover truth and of religion to inculcate piety. Similarly, the aim of national leadership is to strengthen national loyalty. While this distinction is too restrictive for my taste, it points to a hidden truth about the organized approach to morality. It must forever be on guard against lending absolute sanctity to the many proximate moral positions taken by man in society which come near to objective truth but never exhaust it. In American politics, the various constitutional and legislative principles affecting voting rights, property rights, or freedom from search and seizure express and reflect what the Founding Fathers called "The Higher Law" but are not identical with it. Every provisional approach to justice must be measured against justice itself, and the search for justice is the business of the moralist and philosopher. This is why there is always a tension between religion or morality and social behavior—a tension which is not accidental or produced by fuzzy thinking but inherent in the nature of things. The road to disaster lies in the denial both of the realities of social behavior in their context or of ultimate norms.

Politics illustrates the fact of this tension more graphically than other forms of conduct because it touches our lives and consciences at a particularly vulnerable point. Political action is a serious business. It is conduct that is full of cravings and passions. It involves the quest for influence and power and the maintenance of tolerable authority. It is likely to express base as well as noble feelings, hatred and resentment no less than respect for the general welfare. And yet, in the searching words of the French religious philosopher Paul Ricoeur: "The saving factor about politics is that they have to involve responsibility. In the true sense politics are an activity undertaken by responsible men. They are responsible because they are working for a cause, even if that cause is no more than the ambition of a certain group. They are responsible because the public interest and the permanent trend of the nation is ultimately involved. Politics finally becomes respectable because of their decisive, indelible influence on society."[1]

POLITICS AND MORALITY

To say that moralists or philosophers are not responsible in Ricoeur's sense for what they do is merely to point up a difference. Politicians confronted with a serious decision know they must live with the consequences. On the issue at hand, there will never be a second chance. The moralist can reconsider particularly if he has the courage to change his mind. The leader must decide what is feasible in practice; the moralist, what is desirable. That is why the law of politics is never the law of perfection. In Ricoeur's words, "The religious conscience says, 'If thou are not perfect in every respect, thou are not perfect at all.' Politics are never subject to this law; their achievements can never be more than relatively good. That is why the politician is faced by a terrible problem; it is not the problem of maintaining his innocence, but that of *limiting his culpability*."[2]

In these circumstances, the church or the religious man must find the resources to grasp, as it were, both horns of the dilemma. "Being the salt of the earth means the Church must maintain the tension between a morality of absolute right and wrong (the morality of the Gospel) and the morality of what is feasible in practice (the morality of politics)."[3] It must hold to this tension

1   Paul Ricoeur, "Ye Are the Salt of the Earth," *Ecumenical Review*, X (1958), 274.
2   *Ibid.*
3   *Ibid.*

almost to the breaking point. Some have looked for a simple way out by grasping at dogmas of perfection. The philosopher Leonard T. Hobhouse, aware of this tendency, wrote, "The evidence of the truth of an idea is not yet separate from the quality which renders it pleasant." Our wisest religious philosophers have resisted this escape from the stubborn reality of the problem, and one of them asserts: "It would be the greatest hypocrisy if the Christian were to insist on introducing the absolute claims of the Sermon on the Mount directly and brutally into politics, ignoring the tension between such absolute claims and the relative, inadequate possibilities of political action."[4] But while rejecting perfectionism as a simple way out from the dilemmas of politics, the religiously sensitive person must never close his eyes to a higher order of truth. There must be a note of pathos in his defense of an action that he conceives to be politically just, for if he is honest he can never escape the knowledge that his act is not just under all circumstances and especially not ultimately just. This fact explains why men read Lincoln's political utterances today and have forgotten other leaders of the past and present. He was conscious of the inevitable tension between what he did and what he might have desired to do, and he had the courage to say so.

SCIENCE AND MORALITY

Science and particularly its consequences as they relate to morality bear at least a limited resemblance to politics. The scientific method deals with the mechanics of life but not with the qualitative issues. It answers the how and not the why. It provides the circumstances for moral decisions but offers little guidance for decisions themselves. In the same way, the moralist must understand more about politics if he is to speak with any relevance on political morality; he must grasp the conditions introduced and brought about by science. Science, like politics, creates modalities of action. Given its complexities and the rap-

4 *Ibid.*

idly changing scene that it is continually bringing about and within which men must act, science tests moral sensitivity along a changing front. It furnishes new power for good and evil, and the moralist must comprehend this. It provides new knowledge against which ancient maxims must be tested and reinterpreted. In the end, it demands roughly the same kind of on balance judgments so familiar to those who seek to do right in politics.

As distinguished scientists, like Dr. Warren Weaver of the Sloan Foundation, have noted, medical science confronts mankind with a host of new problems arising from the conflict between respect for human life and the possibility of experimentation with a dying man that might save lives in the future. I know of only two philosophers writing about such problems, David Daube of Oxford University and Samuel Stumpf of Vanderbilt. They have considered the moral problems raised by scientific advances from the standpoint of traditional philosophy and the historic questions of philosophers concerned with individual rights, society's interests, and the claims of future generations on present practices. Warren Weaver by contrast views the problem primarily in terms of the scientist's quest for truth, but his thinking is also informed by a deep commitment to Judaeo-Christian values. Dr. Weaver observes: "Suppose a person ill with cancer—with such a type and condition of cancer that the chances are 100 to 1 that the person will be dead within thirty days. Suppose the medical scientists wish to inject live cells of another type of cancer into the body of this person. This procedure has no promise whatsoever of helping the person in question; but it may produce knowledge which will help others."[5] If the patient consents, does the doctor inject the cells? To approach an answer to this baffling question, the moralist has a right to ask further questions. Had the patient full command of his faculties when he consented? Have he and his doctor had the

5   Warren Weaver, "Some Moral Problems Posed by Modern Science," Address to the Washington Colloquium on Science and Society, April 27, 1965, pp. 8–9.

benefit of the best available knowledge on the chances of re-
covery or remission of the cancer, perhaps through a panel of
consulting specialists? Have the factual situation and the limits of
factual knowledge been fully explored and explained to the
patient and his dependents? If all these steps have been taken
and the doctor and the patient have participated in the decision,
with the law being no obstacle, is this an instance in which an
action may be taken to serve a greater good? Religion has grap-
pled in the past with somewhat similar moral issues, and while
its answers have not always been consistent they illustrate the
problem. What course should the doctor follow if mother and
child are endangered in childbirth and one or the other cannot
survive? Roman Catholic moralists place the life of the child
first, but most fathers would choose to safeguard the life of their
wives. Does the motivation of the former tradition stem from
anxiety that some doctors may take the easy way out and under-
value the life of the unborn child? Does the crucial decision both
in childbirth and cancer rest on holding firm to the ultimate
principle of respect for human life up to and slightly beyond the
point where the hard decision of whether to save only one life
. or to serve future generations becomes necessary and justifiable?
Even then, the moralist must ask what the reasonable prospects
are that such an experiment will achieve what less drastic experiments cannot.

Another question concerns the prolonging of human life
through countless artificial means beyond the point when all
hope of life has passed. Is this a case where the law has been
controlling and made doctors reluctant to follow what they considered the most humane course? Is this issue, therefore, one
that must be debated in legislative assemblies and a new consensus achieved? What can one say of the abuse and the absence
of respect for human life involved in perpetuating the suffering
of someone for whom there is utterly no hope of survival? Is
it fair to ask that doctors do justice by violating the law or must
the law be changed? Is this change a matter for the community

as it strives in its wisdom to give doctors authority to act in accordance with their best scientific knowledge? Does it come down to the balancing of two principles involving respect for human life and its abuse or ending? Is there a difference between prolonging a life by stimulating the heart for a few hours compared with preserving another life when the mind is still active and alert though the body is disabled?

There are also the issues raised by increased life expectancy through transplanting human organs and eventually the heart from one person to another. Does this alter the moral entity and a person's behavior as his biological and glandular qualities are altered? Religion would, I believe, assert that the sources of moral conduct are deeper and more profound than the endocrine system. Man's spirit or soul is not a product of particular physiological characteristics or else the crippled or handicapped would not comprise some of our most sensitive human spirits. Moreover, man is forever in the process of becoming. The Greek philosopher Thales wrote that the same man never steps into the same river twice. Both he and the river are continuously changing. I agree that the problem of changes in man through medical procedures should not trouble religion, for everyone is subject to molecular changes no less substantial than those brought about by new organs.

More troublesome is the issue of how we are to consider new life, whether "intelligent" creatures from another planet or life in a test tube. What impact will this have on our concept of man and his place in God's universe? A few simple propositions may help to focus discussion on some of the central issues. First, the threat to a universe with man at its center does not begin with space exploration or human genetics. It has been going on for decades, if not centuries, as the lonely and solitary individual has been forced more and more into the background by the processes of modernization, mass organization of societies, and the growing mechanization and dehumanization of society. Religion and morality have struggled to preserve the integrity of human personality and individual conscience despite the pervasive demands of the giant collectivities that shape existence. We know that it is no longer enough for the conscientious individual to stand aside from the social and political actions of larger communities. This leads to the strange paradox that to safeguard individual rights or moral values, the individual must participate in collective action. To assure that majority rule doesn't blot out individual rights, he must play a role in majoritarian government. To preserve his faith, he must, given the world as it is, temporarily set the purity of his faith to one side. From any simple religious standpoint, his acts must seem scandalous, but is not a passive attitude toward life and its changing problems more scandalous still?

Even the broad realm of social action—slum clearance and housing, help to the sick and the aged, and widening opportunities for the poor and disadvantaged—follows the laws of rational organization. A whole vast machinery of social action has been instituted for these purposes. The religious romanticist or perfectionist may rail against it; but the Christian or Jewish or Moslem realist must find a way to work creatively within it, seizing every opportunity to make it more personal and human. In Paul Ricoeur's phrase: "If he is to give effective help to someone, the Good Samaritan of today has to isolate himself more and more from those he wants to help, through a whole gamut of administrative machinery. The spirit of all these bodies is . . . bound to become abstract and dehumanized, while at the same time it is the condition of their effectiveness."[6] Thus, the Christian who is enjoined to love his neighbor man to man discovers that he must channel his love through an administrative case load. In this collective age, love becomes the knack of discovering the human significance of everything that tends to become a case. "To put it briefly, the purpose of Christian love in the [twentieth] century is to maintain [a] constant tension between the final

---

6   Ricoeur, "Ye Are the Salt of the Earth," 268.

object of social therapy (who is a person) and the methods (which are a system)."[7] The risk is that organized social action will rest content with routines and procedures and settle for aid and comfort to a single form of social need. New forms of poverty and need arise, and the Christian must be the prophetic voice who speaks for mankind in all conditions and needs. His antennae must be alert to new forms of cruelty and violence. Torture, which had been on the wane in the eighteenth century, reappeared in the dogmas of Nazism, Stalinism, and colonialism. Neither modernism nor collective social consciousness assures that overall righteousness is on an ascending curve. While working not as an amateur but as a devoted soldier within the changing structures of a collective age, the morally sensitive individual must know that love and justice transcend all the partial unities of mankind. Even though he picks up signals of what is feasible from the order within which he lives, he must look to a higher order for what is desirable.

Second, God's universe is greater than any human vision of it. This frees us from concern that man is downgraded by the discovery of the "intelligent" creatures or new forms of life. God's world is not earth bound nor can we assume that earthly man is the sole form of God's creation. The mystery of human existence and of its relation to God is too grand and awe-inspiring to limit it to the human species.

Third, some observers among us have greater difficulty with the concept of forming and molding the superior individual. Perhaps it smacks too much of racism as practiced by the Nazis. Moreover, who is to say whether any individual requires what scientists have described as the "injection of memory molecules." I am confident that certain forms of individual improvement are not destructive of the individual's moral integrity. Yet, this is an area to be viewed with considerable reserve and circumspection. There are limits to tinkering with moral identity, and

7   *Ibid.*, 270.

individual choice must be determining. The issue of artificial insemination is troublesome enough without going well beyond it in reconstituting human personality.

In summary, then, there is plainly need for long and serious reflection on religious norms, many of which were designed for a world of sheep and shepherds. The underlying principles are valid, but this will not excuse our contemporaries from striving to make them meaningful and relevant. Man is capable of endangering present and future generations with policies that affect the environment. No amount of moral preachment will free our leaders from being politically responsible. It is essential that in programs which may lead to the pollution of the atmosphere, every effort must be made to control human action. But the measuring rod is the complicated one of balancing present necessity against future consequences. Nuclear testing illustrates the full play of this process. The first responsibility of our leaders remains one of protecting and safeguarding national security. History will hold accountable those who disregard the needs of present generations. National security measures require, however, responsible leaders to look both to present needs and future dangers as they affect generations yet unborn. The nuclear test ban is a rational response to the present and the future, and similar policies will be required as man moves toward the twenty-first century.

CHRISTIANITY, RELIGION AND SOCIAL PROBLEMS

One must point out, in reviewing the problems discussed thus far, that public and international affairs threaten to outstrip all human capacities. Our problems are so complex and efforts to meet them so inconclusive that religious men and women, including Christians, turn away in resignation and despair. It is easier to leave that "dirty business" to secular leaders and seek security and contentment in other areas. The organized Christian community with which some of us would identify has a particularly critical problem in this regard. This arises in part because of the dualism of the Christian outlook. On the one hand, Christianity declares that, because men have a touch of God within them, they cannot rest while suffering and exploitation prevail. We believe that the spirit of God is the source of the ultimate standards of social criticism. To repeat John Milton's classic phrase: "My conscience I have from God and I cannot give it to Caesar." In times past, the sense of an ultimate standard provided man with the impulse to enter the public forum and to join the good fight. De Tocqueville could say of Americans: "To take a hand in the regulation of society and to discuss it is his highest concern. . . . If an American were condemned to confine his activities to his own affairs he would be robbed of one half of his existence." If liberal humanism was one part of the inspiration for this outlook, the Judaeo-Christian perspective was the other.

Yet at the heart of much of Christian and religious thought lurks the opposite view that Caesar's world and God's never meet. Of ancient Rome, Tertullian wrote: "We have for Caesar the image of Caesar which is impressed on the coin, for God, the image of God which is impressed on human beings. Give Caesar his money; give yourself to God." But for Tertullian and some later day prophets, giving oneself to God meant, "I owe . . . no obligation to forum, campus, or senate. I stay awake for no public function. I make no effort to monopolize the platform. I pay no heed to administrative duty." The charge of historians such as Gibbon that Rome's decline and fall was the doing of passive Christians doubtless rests on the notion that the passive attitude of Christians toward social problems destroyed the society's vitality and ability to respond to new challenges.

Again today the age-old problem is posed: are religion and life a unity or do they go their separate ways? More particularly, are religion and our common national and international life related or do they exist in separate, watertight compartments? Virtually every critical viewpoint, like that of Bertrand Russell's *Why I Am Not a Christian*, assumes that Christianity must invariably choose the latter alternative. Russell and his friends attack not the truth or falsity of Christianity but its essential irrelevance. In the same vein, secular writers describing a particularly fruitless international conference in which one pious and moralistic pronouncement follows another frequently compare the atmosphere to that of a church. Christians may be stung by such suggestions, but they have a duty to examine the reasons for contemporaries' finding them plausible.

One reason is doubtless religion's tendency toward perfectionism whenever it enters the realm of public and international affairs. Harold Nicholson has commented that religious people compared with cynics make poor diplomats partly because they are forever talking about absolute principles in what is always a practical art. One example is the assertion that "if all men were Christians there would be no war." Closer to home, Christians rarely indulge themselves in such extravagant claims. Who among us maintains that if all others were Christians there would be no divorce or crime or selfishness? In the everyday world we accept Christians and non-Christians as they are and strive for a better but not a perfect world. No less in the international sphere, Christian principles are guides for the strong and the weak whatever the state of their moral advancement. Christians and non-Christians live under the judgments of God. He has judged us as we judge others. If the world sensed that we believed this as fervently as we believed in our own righteousness, the cries of hypocrisy, self-righteousness, and cant might be silenced. Christianity and religion are indeed relevant to public and world affairs, both to assure a sense of righteousness and justice and to act as a safeguard against self-pride and hypocrisy. Knowing this, those who hold to its truths can act with grace and confidence even in an uncertain and ambiguous realm.